The Campus Green:
Fund Raising in Higher Education

D0882012

by Barbara E. Brittingham and Thomas R. F

ASHE-ERIC Higher Education Report 1, 1990

This report is a special cooperative project between the
Council for the Advancement and Support of Higher Education (CASE)
and the ERIC Clearinghouse on Higher Education

Prepared by

Clearinghouse on Higher Education
The George Washington University

In cooperation with

Association for the Study
of Higher Education

Published by

School of Education and Human Development
The George Washington University

Jonathan D. Fife, Series Editor

Cite as

Brittingham, Barbara E. and Pezzullo, Thomas R. *The Campus Green: Fund Raising in Higher Education.* ASHE-ERIC Higher Education Report No. 1. Washington, D.C.: School of Education and Human Development, The George Washington University, 1990.

Library of Congress Catalog Card Number 90-060889
ISSN 0884-0040
ISBN 0-9623882-8-9

Managing Editor: Bryan Hollister
Manuscript Editor: Barbara Fishel/Editech
Cover design by Michael David Brown, Rockville, Maryland

The ERIC Clearinghouse on Higher Education invites individuals to submit proposals for writing monographs for the *ASHE-ERIC Higher Education Report* series. Proposals must include:
1. A detailed manuscript proposal of not more than five pages.
2. A chapter-by-chapter outline.
3. A 75-word summary to be used by several review committees for the initial screening and rating of each proposal.
4. A vita and a writing sample.

ERIC **Clearinghouse on Higher Education**
School of Education and Human Development
The George Washington University
One Dupont Circle, Suite 630
Washington, DC 20036-1183

This publication was prepared partially with funding from the Office of Educational Research and Improvement, U.S. Department of Education, under contract no. ED RI-88-062014. The opinions expressed in this report do not necessarily reflect the positions or policies of OERI or the Department.

EXECUTIVE SUMMARY

In the last two decades, private support has become increasingly important to American institutions of higher education, yet research on fund raising has lagged behind the expansion of institutional effort.

What Are the Notable Changes and Trends in Fund Raising?

Fund raising in American higher education dates back nearly 350 years, and several historical changes have taken place:

- Traditional church-affiliated and individual and personal solicitation has been replaced with increased direct institutional appeals of an organizational and professional nature.
- The notion of *charity* has been replaced with *philanthropy,* and theories of donors' behavior have changed accordingly.
- While once considered an adjunct to the duties of the president or a few trustees, fund raising has become a central institutional activity.
- Though once limited to independent colleges, fund raising in *public* higher education has become accepted.

The recent past and the foreseeable future will be characterized by more formal and centrally planned fund-raising programs, greater use of marketing principles, broader acceptance of an exchange model of donors' behavior, rather than an entirely altruistic one, and wider competition for private funds from every type of institution, including, most recently, public two-year colleges.

What Are the Implications That Can Be Derived from Research?

Studies of institutional effectiveness using institutional, student, and alumni characteristics and analyses of donors' behavior have dominated research in fund raising for the last 20 years. Although few unqualified generalizations about effectiveness can be made from the literature, a clear and consistent association is found between *dollars spent on fund raising* and *results of fund raising.* But increased spending is not the same as *wisely* increased spending, and little research is available for guidance on how to spend well. Beyond the level of spending, many studies associate success in fund raising with institutional pride, prestige, and emotional attachment by alumni. These results are important to the practitioner, because properly organized advancement programs to enhance pride, prestige, and alumni attachment can be part of a comprehensive strategy to enhance fund raising. Some factors generally associated with successful fund raising, however, are not under the control of the advancement office or readily altered in the interests of fund raising (size, location, historical success in fund raising, and type of governance, for example).

What Is Known about Spending on Fund Raising?
Research on spending has been limited to surveys, providing limited insight into optimum level, relation to output, or control of marginal costs of fund raising. The best informed advice suggests that internal rather than cross-institutional comparisons should be made, with careful attention to monitoring average costs, changes in marginal cost per gift dollar, diminishing returns, the percent of total institutional budget spent on advancement, and gift income by source and program.

What Is Known about the Behavior of Donors?
The more promising models of individuals' behavior as donors depart from models of pure altruism in favor of exchange models, which attempt to explain donors' motives based on receipt of "goods"—perquisites, tokens, or honors—in exchange for the gift, and a repeated disequilibrium that follows, leaving the donor with a need to respond to recognition and acknowledgment with yet more gifts.

In general, people more disposed to giving are religious (especially Protestant), married with children, women, and better educated. Alumni donors tend to be wealthier, be middle-aged or older, have strong emotional ties to their alma maters, have earned at least a bachelor's degree, participate in some alumni activities, and have religious or voluntary affiliations. Sex and marital status are not good predictors of alumni giving. The search for precollege or college variables (including major, place of residence, and participation in student activities) associated with giving has yielded few consistent findings, though having sufficient financial aid, particularly in the form of scholarships, may be related to future giving.

Corporate giving is tied to self-interest, such as gains in

research in the area of the company's needs, production of trained personnel, employees' morale, and the improvement of the community's environment.

Foundations appear most interested in a college's past successes, the evidence of its ability to perform, its size, and its prestige. Highly focused, thinly staffed, and conservative, most foundations are inclined to give to established and larger organizations and may follow the lead of other donors or larger foundations without further research and evaluation.

Donors of all types seem to be aware of the link between price and quality, favoring institutions of prestige and magnitude. Companies and organizations respond conservatively in times of economic setback, while individuals give despite such times. The wealthy are most sensitive to the price of giving, responding to changes in deductibility, while the middle class and the poor—particularly when it comes to church giving—seem unaffected by tax incentives or fluctuations in the economy.

Scant evidence of any substance suggests that success in intercollegiate athletics is associated with increases in giving other than in the most limited time periods or in anecdotal cases.

What Major Ethical Issues Do Fund Raisers Face?

Fund raising is tied fundamentally to an institution's values and priorities, even as it helps shape those values and priorities. Today, fund raisers face difficult questions—relating their energies to their institution's overall priorities, establishing a proper relationship between donors and the institution, determining which information the institution is obliged to share with prospective and actual donors, knowing when a gift should be refused, and determining the obligations of fund raisers to their institutions and the larger community. These issues are made the more difficult because fund raisers operate without the cloak of academic freedom, are often strongly driven by the bottom line, and have few professional opportunities to consider matters of values or ethics with peers from other institutions.

What Does Research on Fund Raising Imply for Practice?

The following recommendations are offered to institutions:

1. Consider sources of private support strategically, deciding which sources have the best potential for a particular

institution.

2. Designate some private support for areas that will build students' understanding of the importance of private support for colleges and universities and may help shape their future behavior as alumni.
3. Work to strengthen institutional traditions of philanthropy and community service.
4. Participate in locally useful research studies with the candid exchange of information among peers.

The following recommendations apply to professional associations and foundations:

1. Broaden professional development conferences and workshops, going beyond the techniques of fund raising and into research findings and discussions of values and ethics.
2. Establish opportunities for reflection and research on practice, such as sabbatical and study leaves and programs for visiting scholars and practitioners.
3. Continue and strengthen the developing support for research in fund raising and efforts to integrate philanthropy into the curriculum.
4. Lead and support institutions in shaping their fund raising to reflect demographic changes.
5. Include research and evaluation as a central focus of professional organizations, their publications, and their meeting programs.

What Focus Is Needed for Future Research?

An Agenda for Research on Fund Raising (Carbone 1986a) provides a concise and exciting focus for research on fund raising. Now, four years after the conference that was the basis for the *Agenda,* the work stands up well as a prescription for strengthening the body of knowledge, making the literature more professional, and addressing the information needs of fund raisers and decision makers in higher education. The extant research literature is both promising and disappointing (Carbone 1986a; Paton 1985). Despite several exciting individual studies, the literature is weakened by too little consistency in the definition of data and approaches to research and a widespread lack of follow-up on initial or exploratory studies that might strengthen and extend or correct the initial efforts.

Some suggested areas for research are offered as they derive from the authors' review of research:

- *Research on spending and the effectiveness of fund raising.* While institutional spending seems associated with greater effectiveness in fund raising, energy needs to be applied to examining the returns on a variety of approaches to increased effort, comparing and contrasting the returns under reasonably comparable conditions and institutional types.
- *Research on consistency of college mission.* In the past 50 years, many institutions have abandoned or substantially modified their historical character. Are the alumni of colleges whose missions have remained consistent more likely to remain loyal and demonstrate their support financially? Are those that have clung to their historic missions missing support from potential new sources while maintaining only traditional ones?
- *Research on formation of alumni donors' attitudes.* The evidence linking the emotional commitment of alumni to their behavior as donors now suggests that more research should be conducted on how those attitudes form, when they form, and the extent to which postgraduation activities can influence those attitudes. If attitudes cannot be changed after graduation through bonding and cultivation, the influence of the undergraduate experience and the focus of alumni advancement will take on increased importance.
- *Evaluation as research.* Program evaluations conducted with research-like rigor can both be useful immediately for decision making and form the basis for broader generalizations for other institutions.

With these guidelines for future inquiry, it will be possible to add crucial information to the development of an integrated theory of fund raising, donors' behavior, and effectiveness of fund raising.

ADVISORY BOARD

CONSULTING EDITORS

Leonard L. Baird
University of Kentucky

James H. Banning
Colorado State University

Trudy W. Banta
University of Tennessee

Margaret J. Barr
Texas Christian University

Louis W. Bender
Florida State University

Rita Bornstein
University of Miami

Larry Braskamp
University of Illinois

L. Leon Campbell
University of Delaware

Robert F. Carbone
University of Maryland

Darrell Clowes
Viginia Polytechnic Institute and State University

Susan Cohen
Lesley College

John W. Creswell
University of Nebraska

Mary E. Dilworth
ERIC Clearinghouse on Teacher Education

James A. Eison
Southeast Missouri State University

Lawrence Erickson
Southern Illinois University

Valerie French
American University

J. Wade Gilley
George Mason University

Jeffrey H. Orleans
Council of Ivy Group Presidents

Wayne Otto
University of Wisconsin

Robert L. Payton
Indiana University

Joseph F. Phelan
University of New Hampshire

James J. Rhatigan
Wichita State University

John E. Roueche
University of Texas

Steven K. Schultz
Westmont College

Mary Ellen Sheridan
Ohio State University

Robert L. Sizmon
Wake Medical Center

William F. Stier, Jr.
State University of New York at Brockport

Betty Taylor
Lesley College

Reginald Wilson
American Council on Education

REVIEW PANEL

Charles Adams
University of Amherst

Richard Alfred
University of Michigan

Philip G. Altbach
State University of New York

Louis C. Attinasi, Jr.
University of Houston

Ann E. Austin
Vanderbilt University

Robert J. Barak
State Board of Regents

Alan Bayer
Virginia Polytechnic Institute and State University

John P. Bean
Indiana University

Louis W. Bender
Florida State University

Deane G. Bornheimer
New York University

Carol Bland
University of Minnesota

John A. Centra
Syracuse University

Arthur W. Chickering
George Mason University

Jay L. Chronister
University of Virginia

Mary Jo Clark
University of Minnesota

Shirley M. Clark
University of Minnesota

Darrel A. Clowes
Virginia Polytechnic Institute and State University

CONTENTS

FOREWORD

Fund-raising efforts on college and university campuses have accelerated over the past two decades. Most institutions are growing increasingly dependent on voluntary support—gifts from alumni, friends, and corporate and business firms. What was once the expert domain of private institutions is now common at public colleges and universities.

Now, more than any other time, thre is a need to understand what motivates the flow of money from private sources. Government support has dropped, and inflation has not risen quickly enough to balance college costs naturally. As voluntary giving has become more important to the survival of academic institutions, more organizations seek donors in more aggressive ways.

Fund raisers, also known as development officers, must devote additional resources to acquiring unrestricted support. Yet when called upon to raise money, development professionals find only a small, uncodified pool of knowledge concerning fund-raising practices. Research on the effectiveness and efficiency of fund-raising techniques lags behind the task.

The Campus Green by Barbara E. Brittingham and Thomas R. Pezzullo provides a comprehensive summary of what research has been done on fund raising. What are the costs of fund raising? What is known of donor motivation? What are the dependency relationships between corporations and foundations and institutions of higher education? What is the connection between successful intercollegiate athletics and successful fund raising? Looking ahead, the authors suggest the directions development practice might take—where will fund raisers look for resources in the next decade, how will they cultivate those resources efficiently, what are the appropriate fund-raising roles for trustees and presidents.

With the commissioning of this entry in the highly visible *ASHE/ERIC/GWU Higher Education Report* Series, the Council for Advancement and Support of Education (CASE) provides advancement officers with a concise picture of the nature and value of development research. The editors at ERIC and CASE are also bringing to the attention of the research community a set of parameters for research in the area. As institutions need to increase voluntary support, development officers will find support in using research to inform policy decisions. Reading Brittingham and Pezzullo's summary and reviewing their suggestions will make for thoughtful and effective practice. A comprehensive annotation of the literature will help researchers from education and other social sciences focus their studies.

As research on fund raising becomes more common, new questions and concerns will be raised. Brittingham and Pezzullo's overview of research on the campus green will help to bring answers to these questions within our reach.

Judy Diane Grace
Director of Research
Council for Advancement and
Support of Higher Education

ACKNOWLEDGMENTS

We are grateful to Jonathan Fife and Christopher Rigaux at
the ERIC Clearinghouse on Higher Education for their encouragement, help, and patience. We are also grateful to Michael
Cerullo for his diligent and efficient reference work, to Ste-
ward LaCasce for his thorough reading of a draft of our report
and his candid advice and commentary, and to Ron Margolin,
who continues to give generously from his vast wine cellar
of ideas and experiences, both vintage and nouveau.

To our four anonymous reviewers: We appreciate your careful readings and your thoughtful comments; our manuscript
is better for your suggestions. We particularly appreciate the
assistance and encouragement, always given with good
humor, of Judy Diane Grace of the Council for Advancement
and Support of Education. This work benefited greatly from
her help.

All royalties from the sale of this work
are deposited in a scholarship endowment
in the University of Rhode Island Foundation
in the loving memory of

Ines Rose Longo
Tom Pezzullo, Jr.
and
Eva Stuebe

to whose memories this work is also dedicated.

INTRODUCTION

> *Don't give advice; give money.*
> —Gary Schiffman, student speaker at 1984 commencement
> (SUNY–Binghamton), quoting his uncle,
> with an envelope in hand

In recent years, the challenge of raising private funds has
become increasingly important for both public and private
institutions of higher education. Yet the practice of fund raising is thinly informed by research that can lead to greater
effectiveness, help institutions understand the role fund raising plays in higher education, or illuminate the dilemmas it
presents to practitioners and institutional leaders. Indeed,
many experts view the prospect of effective research on fund
raising rather dimly, citing either the inherent difficulties in
conducting research on human subjects with complex motivations or the problems of serious and well-intentioned
scholars who try to work with practitioners who doubt the
value of research or find no place for it in their professional
agendas. For many practitioners in fund raising:

> *. . . fund raising is more art than science and is likely to
> remain so. No matter how hard we try to be analytical and
> systematic, we cannot gainsay the fact that ours is a pro-
> fession based on transactions among human beings; for
> that reason, among others, it is impossible to subject the basic
> causal relationships in fund raising to rational analysis.
> In the case of many large gifts, for example, the gestation
> period takes several years and the causal chains are intri-
> cate. Almost always they include some factors that we can-
> not know or do not understand and others that, although
> we may perceive them more or less clearly, we cannot influ-
> ence. . . . Fund raising is charged with emotion. That is not
> to deny that there are rational components in the decisions
> donors make but rather to say that almost always powerful
> emotional factors are also involved—so powerful that almost
> every major gift transaction is* sui generis. *Very few gener-
> alizations about them will stand up, either in describing
> what occurred or in predicting what might happen* (Smith
> 1981, p. 61).

A noted author and researcher on fund raising takes a
slightly different, but no less pessimistic, view about the quantity of competent research done and the likelihood that much
more will be done in the near term:

The frustrating limits of current practical knowledge and understanding about development productivity per se and impacts of gift potential in particular reflect features of the development profession as well as the modest popularity of fund raising as a subject of academic research. . . . Justifiable defensiveness and outright skepticism limit professional enthusiasm about participating in empirical inquiries conducted by the few academic researchers who have attempted to study institutional advancement (Paton 1985, p. 44).

Furthermore, he notes:

The majority of other research about development efforts reflects the nearly exclusive prescriptive emphasis of the professional development literature. Many studies examine the relative effectiveness of alternative fund-raising practices in an attempt to identify optimal strategies and techniques. However, these studies confront the common frustration of limited knowledge and understanding about relevant institutional differences that promote or inhibit the productivity of fund-raising efforts, independent of the effectiveness of the specific techniques employed (Paton 1986, p. 34).

"Up to now, . . . research on fund raising has been only sporadic, scatter-gun, and often pedestrian" (Carbone 1986a, p. 22).

Despite these observations, the authors of this monograph undertook a review of the research and scholarly literature on educational fund raising in the United States. Consistent with the opinions and predictions expressed by Smith, Paton, and Carbone, they found a relatively small body of professionally conducted research that could contribute to predictive generalizations. While the number of journal articles pertinent to this project is small, the number of doctoral dissertations examining aspects of fund raising has grown in recent years. Unfortunately, these dissertations often have not been translated into the journals or programs routinely listed by the ERIC Clearinghouse on Higher Education, nor do many authors of dissertations on fund raising appear to pursue subsequent research on the topic. Few professionals who complete a dissertation on fund raising seek careers as scholars; rather, they are committed to careers in educational fund raising and do little more research once the dissertation is complete. The opportunity to publish the findings in a scholarly journal has far less professional importance to a professional fund raiser than, say, to a new professor of higher education.

One can be optimistic about the future, however. Scholars and higher education centers at Indiana University–Purdue University at Indianapolis, Duke University, Yale University, the City College of New York, the University of Maryland, and Case Western Reserve University have recently begun to focus on philanthropy and fund raising. In addition, the Independent Sector in Washington, D.C., has been tracking academic centers and research and convening scholars on a wide range of topics related to fund raising and its societal context. Together, these efforts show considerable promise for future research and scholarship to inform fund-raising practices in higher education.

THE AMERICAN EDUCATIONAL TRADITION
OF PRIVATE PHILANTHROPY

*If we nourish not Larning both church and commonwealth
will sinke. . . . God hath bestowed upon you a bounty full bless-
ing; now if you should please to imploy but one mite of that
greate welth which God hath given, to erect a school of larning,
a college among us; you should due a more glorious work,
acceptable to God and man; and the commemeration of the
first founder of the means of Larning, would be a perpetuat-
ing of your name and honour among us.*
—John Eliot, in a letter requesting money from a wealthy
Englishman, c. 1633

Private support . . . can best be understood in the context of America's voluntary traditions: voluntary service, voluntary association, and voluntary giving.

Private support of American higher education, one of its most
distinctive aspects, can best be understood in the context of
America's voluntary traditions: voluntary service, voluntary
association, and voluntary giving. The traditions of philanthropy, of giving freely for a public good, influence not only
higher education in America but also charity, humanitarian
reform, social service, environmental protection, foreign aid,
religion, health, and the arts. Institutionally, philanthropy is
part of America's voluntary or independent sector, sometimes
called "the third sector" (the other sectors, each of which has
important links to philanthropy, are business [or for-profit],
government, and family [or informal]) (Douglas 1983; Gurin
and Van Til 1989).

The roots of philanthropy have been traced to about 4000
B.C., when Egypt's Book of the Dead praised those who fed
the hungry and gave water to those who thirsted (Gurin and
Van Til 1989). Notions of charity and good deeds are also
found in the Old Testament. The beginnings of educational
fund raising can be found more than 2,000 years ago, in the
fourth century B.C., when Plato directed that after his death
the income from his fields be used to support the Academy.
This reference appears to be the earliest record of a gift to
education as well as the earliest example of a bequest and
an endowment. Centuries later, in England in 1601, the new
Statute of Charitable Uses, representing the origins of public
regulation of charity and philanthropy, permitted giving to
charitable causes.

American philanthropy as we know it is a European import,
developed from European traditions and institutions and
often, in colonial times, nurtured with contributions from
European donors. Yet the real founders of American philan-

---

thropy, those who began its special flavor, are the "men and women who crossed the Atlantic to establish communities that would be *better* than, instead of like or different from, the ones they had known at home" (Bremner 1988, p. 7).

What began as charity motivated by religious beliefs soon broadened to a general concern for the quality of life. Cotton Mather, often remembered for his role in the witchcraft trials, was an early American thinker and writer on philanthropy. A founder of Yale University, Mather introduced the notions of pleasure from helping others and of a life of good deeds' increasing the likelihood of success in business. Benjamin Franklin broadened the American notion of giving to include secular concerns: Seeking neither patents for nor profits from his inventions, he made their use available to the world at large. Franklin also broadened the concepts of philanthropy by founding a volunteer fire department, emphasizing giving that would prevent rather than alleviate poverty, and helping to found the American Philosophical Society, the first American association for promoting research in the natural and social sciences (Bremner 1988).

Today, charity connotes serving the poor, while philanthropy "takes a more impersonal and dispassionate approach to bettering the human condition by institutionalizing giving, focusing beyond the immediate condition of people on root causes of human problems and systematic reform, recognizing a responsibility to the public interest, and helping to effect social change" (Gurin and Van Til 1989, p. 3). While notions of giving are considered universal among human societies, philanthropy is distinctively strong in America for reasons that have been associated with religious tradition, democracy, pluralism, and the nurturing of individual effort.

Early American Origins and Church Support
Educational fund raising in America began in 1641, when the Massachusetts Bay Colony sent three clergymen back to England to raise money to support Harvard College, making it possible for Harvard to continue to "educate the heathen Indian." One of them returned from England within a year with 500 pounds for the college and the colony, and the others sent back word that they needed "literature" that would outline the best "selling points of New England." The product was *New England's First Fruits,* the forerunner of case statements and fund-raising brochures. In 1644, the New England

Confederation of four colonies recommended that each family within the confederation contribute a shilling or a peck of wheat for scholarships to Harvard.

The custom of solicitation in Great Britain for college fund raising continued for almost a century to support the nine colleges developed during the colonial period, and as close to the Revolution as 1754, Princeton still dispatched solicitors to England. The fund raising continued in England and briefly in France until the chilling effects of the colonies' political behavior undermined the mother country's largesse.

Benjamin Franklin not only participated in fund raising during his lifetime, playing the lead role in the founding and financing of Philadelphia College (which was to become the University of Pennsylvania), but also established several endowments to further advance his efforts after his death.

Many early American institutions were as likely named for an actual or potential benefactor as they might be for founders:

- Rev. John Harvard gave 779 pounds and a library to the college that was to be his namesake;
- Elihu Yale's initial gift to Collegiate School in Connecticut was a modest shipment of goods from England;
- Nicholas Brown provided $160,000 to the College of Rhode Island;
- Benjamin Franklin's gift of 1,000 pounds enabled the establishment of the Pennsylvania college that would later bear his name along with John Marshall's;
- Charles Tufts gave land;
- Henry Rutgers gave a bell and $5,000 to the trustees of then Queens College;
- The Colgates gave from their fortunes sufficiently to be honored with a renaming of Madison University; and
- Waterville College honored Gardner Colby appropriately after he bailed it out of financial disaster.

One institution stands out in contrast: the University of Chicago, which does not bear the name of John D. Rockefeller, despite his founding gift of $600,000 in 1889 and subsequent gifts totaling $80 million from his heirs and trustees.

By the time of the Civil War, almost 200 colleges existed in the United States, most of them dependent on an affiliated religious denomination for financial support, which in turn depended on donations. The colleges produced a literate citizenry—and clergymen—and helped to spread the denomination's moral values.

Colleges that admitted women or were established exclusively for women likewise depended on individual founding donations or the continuing philanthropy of many individuals. Likewise, the establishment of the earliest black colleges was made possible by benefactors bearing the names of Rockefeller, Carnegie, and Morgan.

What we think of as modern or novel gift instruments are themselves quite long established. Even gifts of annuity date back as far as 1839, when Azariah Williams deeded a piece of land valued at $250,000 to the University of Vermont with the stipulation that he receive annual income from the gift until his death.

The Annual Alumni Fund

[The university should] . . . hope that the men she had been sending forth into the honorable callings and professions might testify to their indebtedness to the University by increasing her power and usefulness. . . . Let it not be thought that the aid furnished by the State leaves no room for munificence.
—James Angell, president of the University of Michigan in his 1871 inaugural statement

Not all funds were raised to establish or salvage fledgling institutions or for a long-lasting purpose. Broad-based, small annual gift programs for current needs have been around for a hundred years, when alumni solicitation began. Records of alumni giving date to the 17th century. The first formal association of graduates of a collegiate institution dates back to 1821 at Williams College and was called the Society of Alumni. The oldest alumni *fund* was established at Yale in 1890, and with just under 400 alumni participating, $11,000 was raised. Early imitators were Princeton, Amherst, Dartmouth, and Cornell. In 1905, Harvard's alumni responded to a call for help from President Eliot and raised $2.5 million to augment faculty salaries in the liberal arts.

Despite the many early associations and annual funds, in 1936 a survey of American colleges reported that fewer than half the institutions surveyed reported having an annual alumni fund (Pray 1981, p. 1). Today it is difficult to find many established four-year colleges that have not organized an annual giving program aimed at its graduates. Most recently, they have been joined by community and junior colleges.

Charitable Gifts from Business Gains

Although individual giving remains the single most important source of private support, corporate gifts and sponsorships and gifts from foundations constitute a significant source of support for higher education. According to the Council for Aid to Education (formerly the Council for Financial Aid to Education), in 1987–88, *individuals* gave an estimated $3.97 billion (48.4 percent of the total private voluntary support of higher education) to colleges and universities, and corporations and foundations gave an estimated $3.46 billion (42.2 percent of the total) (1989, p. 3).

Before the 1950s, corporate support was relatively undocumented, largely because the concepts of giving money away and corporate philanthropy were not perceived to be what business was about. The only available estimate of support from both corporations and foundations suggests that their support constituted less than 6 percent of the total of higher education's private support during the 1950s, a likely result of their understandable resistance to making gifts from profits. Both practice and philosophy dictated that one would not, and perhaps could not, disperse funds from the corporation without a logical and direct benefit to the corporation. Some of the few companies that did make significant gifts to higher education were met with vocal challengers. In 1953, the Supreme Court of New Jersey, in *A.P. Smith Manufacturing Company* v. *Barlow et al.,* upheld "the legality of an unrestricted corporate gift to Princeton University," an action that had been challenged by the stockholders (Allem 1968; Meyer 1971). The court, noting the widespread public belief in the importance of nongovernmental institutions of learning, said that "corporations have come to recognize [it] and with their enlightenment have sought to insure and strengthen the society [that] gives them existence" (Meyer 1971, p. 28).

During the fifties, simultaneous with the growth in all other sources of financial support for higher education, corporate gifts—more likely called "support"—became a significant source of dollars for higher education. Corporate donations, which were officially nonexistent until 1935, increased to $38 million in 1940, $70 million in 1953, $950 million in 1970

(Ishoy 1972), and $1.85 billion in 1988, or about 23 percent of all private voluntary support of higher education (Council for Aid 1989).

Corporate profits can become charitable gifts (limited by law since 1935 to 5 percent of pretax net income but increased to 10 percent in 1981) in several ways. Some company profits become gifts through the company owner's or management's donations to their personal favorite charity. Some wealthy individuals and large profitable corporations have formed charitable foundations for the purpose of administering the distribution of funds transferred from the company to the foundation, assisted by a professional staff, while still others have a program for charitable giving administered by a department established for that purpose. Much corporate giving is also seen as a fringe benefit to employees, when the employer matches individuals' charitable gifts or when the gifts indirectly benefit the employees by improving the community or offering educational opportunities to employees' dependents.

Some companies make gifts of surplus equipment or from the inventory of their own manufactured goods. Their motivation need not be entirely altruistic, because their corporate identification goes along with the gift and the public's identification of the company's name with its charitable objective enhances its image.

Corporations can also support college activities through a vehicle known as "cause-related advertising" or "cause-related marketing." Controversial in many settings, such activities may be most troublesome on college campuses, when, for example, producers of alcoholic beverages seek to buy visibility for their name, product logo, or advertisement, often in association with athletic activities.

Whatever the method, corporate altruism is bolstered by the tax advantages of giving and by enhancing its image through good will that reflects favorably on the organization.

The late 19th and early 20th century industrialization of America led to the development of great fortunes unweakened by income tax. One by-product was the establishment of foun-

dations. Carnegie[1] and Rockefeller developed the earliest and
most sustained models for giving to higher education from
business gains: a focus on larger and research-oriented institutions, medical education, and social service and a diminution of support for religion. Their foundations were established to be "capable of distributing private wealth with
greater intelligence and vision than the donors themselves
could hope to possess" (Bremner 1988, p. 115). The earliest
efforts of these foundations were not uniformly welcomed
in higher education, however, and during the early years of
the Carnegie Corporation and the Rockefeller Foundation,
many individuals decried the influence of the monied on
education.

Carnegie's efforts to establish a national system of pensions
for professors (what has become TIAA) was held up to scru-
tiny and suspicion as a means of influencing professors'
thoughts and undermining the relationship between colleges
and their sponsoring religious denominations. Some of the
early foundations may have been overly controlled by their
founder/donor parent corporation and as a consequence
viewed with skepticism. Sometimes their motives were considered more base than altruistic, characterizing their philanthropy "as a form of baronial self-indulgence" (Nielsen 1985,
p. 21). As time passed and the founders died, independent
trustees drawn from more diverse backgrounds helped to
reduce—but not eliminate—this suspicion.

Some of the charitable overtures of the Rockefeller Foundation in the 1920s were rebuffed as a gesture to resist
monopolistic controls. The suspicion and reluctance continued even into the 1930s, but since World War II, foundations' support for higher education has emerged as an important and reliable source of funds. Today, approximately 23,600
foundations are active in the United States, with total assets
of $64.5 billion, or roughly half the total assets of the country's
400 wealthiest people. The foundations' support for higher
education in 1988 was approximately 19.6 percent (or $1.6
billion) of total private support for higher education, behind

1. Carnegie chose to administer his philanthropy himself and before his death
had distributed more than $300 million. His 1889 "Gospel of Wealth" outlined
his philosophy and motivation: " . . . the surplus [that] accrues from time
to time in the hands of a man should be administered by him in his own
lifetime for that purpose which is seen by him, as trustee, to be best for the
good of the people" (Carnegie 1900, p. 48).

individual sources (48.4 percent) and corporations (23 percent or $1.85 billion) (Council for Aid 1989, p. 3).

Today, like the presence of an alumni association and an annual fund, soliciting gifts from corporations and foundations and accepting corporate sponsorships are as common on most campuses as the computer center or the student union. American higher education not only welcomes private voluntary support from all sources but also depends on it for quality, diversity, and, in many cases, survival.

Professional Fund Raising and Fund-Raiser Organizations

World War I challenged this country to "make the world safe for democracy," and our participation was supported in part by "individual subscriptions to the greatest fund-raising drives yet known in history" (Ishoy 1972, p. 83). In a drive organized in May 1917, the American Red Cross raised over $114 million to support European war relief in eight days in June, making history in fund raising. It also raised $100 million a year later and $169 million in another eight-day drive in 1918. On the eve of the armistice, the first United Fund Drive raised over $203 million in 15 days, the largest sum that had ever been raised through voluntary offerings.

The successful fund raising in World War I led to the founding of professional fund-raising firms. Charles Ward, a fund raiser for the YMCA, and Harvey J. Hill opened Ward and Hill Associates in 1919. The five largest fund-raising firms in the United States today have their origins with that firm. Shortly after its founding, Ward and Hill added Lyman Pierce and F. Herbert Wells and became Ward, Hill, Pierce & Wells. Other partners joined them in the next few years: Arnaud Marts, George Lundy, Bayard M. Hedrick, George Tamblyn, Olaf Gates, Christian H. Dreshman, and Herman F. Reinhardt. Arnaud Marts served as president of Bucknell at the same time he was president of Marts and Lundy.

John Price Jones worked in private fund raising and was recruited after World War I to work for Harvard, his alma mater, heading the Harvard Endowment Fund Campaign. He established a public relations campaign and "sought to develop enthusiasm for giving to Harvard by dignified means rather than employ any rough and tumble methods" (Ishoy 1972, p. 89). The publicity thus generated reflected the nature of the institution, and potential donors were given reasons to support the institution. Jones's efforts were successful and he surpassed the goal of $10 million, raising $14.2 million for the 1919 campaign. Subsequently, he founded the John Price Jones fund-raising company.

The difficulty of raising money in hard economic times led some fund raisers to use high pressure or unscrupulous techniques. Partly in response to this situation, nine of the major long-standing fund-raising firms joined together and in 1935 formally founded the American Association of Fund-Raising Counsel. They met from time to time for 20 years as an informal group to talk shop and discuss professional ethics. In 1955, they hired an executive director and opened a New York office, and by 1970, the AAFRC had over 25 member firms and promulgated its Fair Practice Code to guide and determine its membership.

Today, professional fund-raising organizations—fund-raising counsel, as they are called—serve colleges and universities through consultation on the design and conduct of fund raising, feasibility studies, and development of case statements for campaigns; conduct internal audits or studies of organization and readiness; and offer on-site fund-raising management services.[2]

Overall Trends
From the origins of private voluntary support in the 17th century to the 1980s, several trends are noteworthy:

1. *The wide shift away from church-affiliated and individual and personal solicitation to direct institutional appeals of an organizational and professional nature.* Colleges and universities once depended on clergy to solicit funds from the pulpit in supporting church-affiliated schools for their value to the denomination. Today, most established colleges have organized, professional development staffs that reach well beyond individual and direct-constituent fund raising.
2. *The dramatic shift away from the notion of* charity *and toward* philanthropy. The emphasis, particularly in fund raising from other than alumni, is on investment or the

2. See Ishoy 1972, Korvas 1984, and Sherratt 1975 for a more detailed and complete history.

value of the gift in noncharitable terms: the impact of independent educational institutions on society, the quid pro quo value to corporations and other organizations, the tax advantages to the wealthy and to corporations in making gifts, and the focus on exchange, whereby a donor gets a sense of influencing educational policy, or on research or on merely helping to preserve the independence of the institution.

3. *The imposing role fund raising plays in all aspects, daily or yearly, of institutional life rather than being limited to crises or major changes in direction.* Earliest fund raising stressed the preservation of fragile institutions; more modern approaches stress strengthening already stable and vital organizations or the opportunity to extend the value of the institution to new clientele, students, or geographies integral to the comprehensive and strategic planning of modern institutions.

4. *The widespread acceptance of fund raising among state-assisted colleges and universities in the last 40 years.* Fund raising, which was based more heavily on charity in the early years, was understandably concentrated in schools that had charitable parent organizations, namely, churches. State-assisted schools were seen as having the support of the sovereign and therefore as ineligible for private support, or the institutions themselves saw it as unnecessary. As pressures have mounted within the institutions for new sources of funding, however, public institutions have borrowed the techniques and methods of the private institutions.

Fund Raising Today

Voluntary support for colleges and universities has become increasingly important to a range of institutions. To some, voluntary support provides resources for survival; for most, it has become a source of discretionary income that can support vitality, innovation, and excellence.

Estimates indicate that about 9,000 full-time fund raisers are employed at colleges and universities in the United States and Canada (Fisher 1989). Based on a survey of members of the Council for Advancement and Support of Education (CASE), the modal fund-raising professional in higher education is male (60 percent), white (97 percent), between 31 and 40 years old (43 percent), has a master's degree (61 percent), is in the first or second year of service in his current position (55 percent), and works in a private institution (60 percent) (Carbone 1987).

Development staff at an institution can range from one person who raises funds part time to 200 or more professional and support staff. Central to most fund-raising offices is the annual fund soliciting alumni and others, including the institution's faculty and staff, friends and members of the community, and parents of current students. A key adjunct to the annual fund for most institutions is a corporate matching program that increases the value of individual donations by a factor of two, sometimes three or more.

Standard additional components of contemporary fund-raising offices include a corporate and foundation relations office or officer to coordinate proposals and appeals to such sources, an office or officer of planned giving to work on arrangements like bequests, trusts, and insurance policies, and a research office to develop and review files on prospective individual, corporate, and foundation donors. Some institutions also have staff designated to work with "major gifts."

Larger or more complex institutions may include development officers with partial or total responsibility to specific parts of the institution as part of a constituency fund-raising operation. Such officers may have responsibility to raise support for athletics, for the liberal arts college or professional schools and colleges, for the library, or for special areas, such as fine arts or health programs. In centralized systems, these constituency fund raisers work out of, report to, or work closely with an institutional development office; in a decentralized system, constituency fund raisers may have little formal relationship with the institutionwide development office.

Data collected each year from participating institutions by the Council for Aid to Education represent the best estimates of total support by source and for each type of institution. Overall, these estimates indicate that private support represents 6.7 percent of total institutional expenditures (Council for Aid 1989). Comparing data from schools that report in multiple years also provides useful estimates of change. Table 1 shows total support for higher education, by source, for 1987–88.

The most recent data from the Council highlight two aspects of current private support: (1) By type, research/doc-

TABLE 1

VOLUNTARY SUPPORT FOR HIGHER EDUCATION, 1987-88

Source	Millions of Dollars	Percent
Alumni	$2,042	24.9%
Nonalumni	1,927	23.5
Corporations	1,853	22.6
Foundations	1,607	19.6
Religious organizations	197	2.4
Other	574	7.0
Total	**$8,200**	**100.0%**

Source: Council for Aid 1989.

TABLE 2

VOLUNTARY SUPPORT BY TYPE OF INSTITUTION
1987-'88 AND CHANGE FROM 1986-'87
(000)

Type of Institution	No.	Voluntary Support in 1987-'88		Percent Change from 1986-87
		Amount	*Average per Institution*	
Research/doctoral				
Private	71	$2,536,522	$35,726	-3.3
Public	112	2,142,948	19,133	+2.4
Comprehensive				
Private	191	617,550	3,233	-13.8
Public	154	212,668	1,381	+7.0
Liberal Arts				
Private	336	1,070,624	3,186	-12.6
Public	12	15,413	1,284	+8.2
Specialized				
Private	99	241,565	2,440	-2.6
Public	17	135,578	7,975	+3.6
Total four-year				
Private	697	$4,466,261	$6,408	-7.1
Public	295	2,506,607	8,497	+2.8
Two-year				
Private	25	19,731	789	-4.6
Public	125	48,685	389	+23.3
All private	722	$4,485,992	$6,213	-7.1
All public	420	2,555,292	6,084	+3.1
Grand total	1,142	$7,041,284	$6,166	-3.7

Source: Council for Aid 1989.

toral institutions raise the most private support, about two-thirds of the total; and (2) within type, private institutions raise more money, on average, than their public counterparts. The type of institution making the greatest percentage gains in fund raising is the public two-year institution. Overall, among institutions that report their data, private institutions now raise 64 percent of total private support (Council for Aid 1989). Table 2 is a summary of total private support, by type of institution, with changes from 1986–87 to 1987–88 shown for the (88 percent of) institutions reporting data for both years.

A comparison of fund-raising programs in a representative group of 73 public and private institutions confirms that private institutions make a greater investment in and have longer histories of seeking private support (Duronio, Loessin, and Borton 1988b). In the survey, the total institutional budget of the 36 public colleges averaged 11 percent higher than the total budget for the 37 private colleges. At the private institutions, however, the average endowment was three and one-half times greater, the annual fund-raising expenses were 57 percent higher, and the total external support for the most recent year was 48 percent higher.

The modal public institution reported less than 10 years of experience in formal programs of seeking support from alumni, nonalumni individuals, corporations, and foundations; the modal private institution reported 10 to 25 years of experience in seeking funds from each of those constituencies (Duronio, Loessin, and Borton 1988b). Extensive involvement of the president and trustees in fund raising was more common among private institutions, but minimal or no involvement of faculty in fund raising was equally likely at either type of institution (64 percent overall).

Colleges and universities conduct capital campaigns to raise large amounts of money for specific purposes, generally including endowments, and to give focus and visibility to increasingly ambitious plans for raising private support. Capital campaigns are the most frequent occasion to bring in outside consultants, often to help with a feasibility study to help set the target, and are typically accompanied by an increase in the number of fund-raising staff.

Described as "a time to attempt the unusual—but not the startling" (Bennett and Hays 1986, p. 16), capital campaigns have been used to plan for and achieve ever higher levels of private giving. In 1960, Harvard's goal of $82 million seemed ambitious; by 1969, the University of Chicago had raised $160.5 million in three years. By the end of the 1970s, 42 percent of small independent colleges had conducted a capital campaign within the last three years, and 72 percent had planned one in the next three (Willmer 1980). By the mid-1980s, 94 percent of colleges under 1,000 students reported they had engaged in a capital campaign (Glennon 1985).

Throughout the 1970s and 1980s, increasing numbers of institutions, including expanding numbers of public institutions, conducted capital campaigns. By 1988, more than 65 colleges and universities were trying to raise $100 million or more within five years, and by 1990, goals of $1 billion were still unusual but no longer startling. Originally discrete events, capital campaigns have become a constant state for some institutions; they serve as a way to describe, package, and communicate the next round of searching for private gifts as well as a vehicle for involving the campus community in the establishment of priorities and the solicitation of support.

INSTITUTIONAL EFFECTIVENESS, POLICIES, AND PROGRAMS

*In the first place I advise you to apply to all those whom you
know will give something; next, to those whom you are uncer-
tain whether they will give anything or not, and show them
the list of those who have given; and lastly, do not neglect those
whom you are sure will give nothing, for in some of them you
may be mistaken.*
—Benjamin Franklin

Institutional effectiveness in fund raising has been the subject
of considerable investigation, but with a variety of methodo-
logical approaches and definitions of effectiveness. Fund raisers, presidents, and governing boards have obvious interests
in determining which program characteristics, techniques,
or patterns of organization are associated with increased effectiveness: Programs of demonstrated effectiveness can be
added, organizational patterns known to increase private giving adopted. Yet some characteristics used in studies of the
effectiveness of fund raising, such as the location of the institution or its proximity to major corporations or foundations,
are not readily subject to change by an act of the administration, the board, or the alumni volunteers. Other variables that
have been used in some studies to predict effectiveness are
more properly thought of as consequences or measures of
effectiveness (e.g., size of the endowment). Knowing their
association with effectiveness may improve one's understanding of effectiveness but add not a whit to one's ability to control it. Advising a college president to increase the size of the
endowment as a way to improve the effectiveness of fund raising is no advice at all.

Three general approaches have been used to study institutional effectiveness in fund raising: (1) studies of *perceived
effectiveness,* (2) studies of *objectively defined effectiveness,*
and (3) studies of *effectiveness adjusted for potential.* In the
first category, researchers employ an operational definition
of effectiveness derived by an expert panel, by the relative
frequency with which practitioners cite a particular charac-
teristic in a survey, or through correlational analysis of institutional characteristics. Such studies often attempt to determine the characteristics of effective fund-raising programs
through surveys of institutions with (or without) regard to
the institution's effectiveness, calling for the staff's professional
judgment about which factors are most significantly related
to effectiveness. Sometimes the studies employ juries of

acclaimed fund raisers, asking them to rate or rank an exhaustive list of program characteristics for their relative importance in an effective program. Several problems are inherent in this approach: (1) What is commonplace or the norm in practice may be vestigial but never *optimal* practices handed down by the folklore of the profession; (2) what was effective years ago may be less so—or even ineffective—today but has not yet dropped from the conventional wisdom; and (3) what is effective for institutions with one set of characteristics may not be as effective for other types of institutions.

The second category of studies, those using objectively defined effectiveness, are more useful and somewhat more generalizable in their findings. Such studies describe and differentiate institutional practices, having made an a priori and objective identification of effective versus ineffective institutions. This objective determination is based on the total amount of support raised, sometimes adjusted for the size of the institution or number of alumni; measures of effectiveness include total dollars raised, or average gift per solicitation, or size of endowment, or endowment dollars per FTE (full-time equivalent) student or per FTE faculty member— or a combination of these and other institutional data. The logic behind this sort of definition is that dollars raised (however scaled or adjusted) is the best proxy of institutional effectiveness in fund raising. This approach has the advantage of identifying institutions, usually on a scale from highly effective to relatively ineffective, and weighting the responses of those institutions' staffs accordingly. A major problem with this approach is that dollars raised, however scaled for institutional differences, cannot account for an institution's position relative to its *potential.* In other words, this approach takes into account neither the institution's potential for fund raising nor its relative effectiveness in raising funds.

The third category of studies includes effectiveness adjusted for potential. More useful conceptually than studies of perceived effectiveness or objectively defined effectiveness, these studies include a measure of the institutions' potential for fund raising and scale effectiveness accordingly. Most commonly, designers of these studies adjust the rating of effectiveness by calculating the percentage of potential actually realized in the fund-raising results, an adjustment not unlike handicapping in horseracing or golf. The logic behind this approach is that an institution with high potential for fund raising and only moderate effectiveness might raise more actual dollars and therefore seem more effective than an institution with a low potential and a rather high effectiveness. When the results are scaled according to their own potential, it is the latter institution rather than the former that will appear more effective. The challenge in this approach is developing and validating useful measures of an institution's potential for raising private support.

The research to date on institutional effectiveness in fund raising includes one large-scale recent study (using objectively defined measures of success) and several smaller studies (of various methodologies and definitions of success), often on particular types of institutions. Taken together, these studies provide some broad indications of factors related to institutional success and begin to paint a picture of complexity, according to institutional type, history, and particular circumstance.

With support from the Exxon Education Foundation, a research team collected data from over 300 institutions and examined their success in raising funds, overall and from four sources (Duronio, Loessin, and Borton 1988a, 1988b; Loessin, Duronio, and Borton 1987, 1988a, 1988b). Institutions included research universities, doctoral universities, comprehensive universities, baccalaureate colleges, and two-year colleges. The results of their regression analyses predicting total support and support from four sources are summarized in table 3.

TABLE 3

PREDICTORS OF SUCCESS IN FUND RAISING, BY SOURCE OF FUNDS

	Alumni	Nonalumni	Corporations	Foundations	Total
Institutional type		X	X	X	X
Enrollment		X	X		X
Size of endowment	X	X	X	X	X
Alumni of record	X		X	X	
Expenditures for fund raising	X		X	X	X
Expenditure per student	X	X	X	X	
Institutional budget		X	X	X	X
Variance explained	**87%**	**69%**	**81%**	**73%**	**87%**

Source: Loessin, Duronio, and Borton 1988b.

For all types of institutions, total voluntary support was most highly correlated (.78–.73) with expenditures for fund raising, institutional budget, and size of endowment. Moderate correlations (.68–.58) were found with number of alumni of record, type of institution, expenditures per student, and enrollment. Low correlations (.28–.12) were found with the age of the institution, tuition, and private or public status.

While the effectiveness in fund raising overall and for all institutions can be related to variables such as size of endowment and expenditures per student, examining institutions by type and donors by source shows considerable variation from the overall pattern, with the greatest variation from the general pattern found among public institutions, as a type, and foundations, as a source (Duronio, Loessin, and Borton 1988b). Thus, while many of the beliefs about the effectiveness of fund-raising practices have come from the longer experience of private institutions, particularly older and wealthier private institutions, their practices are not entirely appropriately generalized to other types of institutions.

In general, the success of an institution's fund-raising program appears related to three types of variables: capacity, history, and effort.

An institution's capacity may be thought of as the hypothetical maximum private support an institution could raise under the best conditions. Capacity for fund raising is partly a function of the size of its alumni body and the collective wealth of its alumni. Older and larger institutions and institutions that attract students from wealthy families or prepare students for high-paying careers have a larger pool of alumni wealth from which they can potentially attract donations. Well-developed alumni ties to corporations and foundations and trustees' leadership in giving tend to increase an institution's capacity for fund raising (Pickett 1977). Capacity may also refer to the institution's total resources, measured, for example, by total expenditures per student or the importance of research in the institution's mission; many donors prefer giving to build on success or to associate with prestige, which they interpret as quality, rather than to fix a deficiency or to give to needier institutions.

Although several researchers have included location or geographic variables in their studies, the results have tended to be inconclusive. Perhaps the clue to the influence of location is a measure of regional economic growth (Leslie and Ramey

1988). And specialized institutions may have particular characteristics that relate to capacity; for example, among church-related schools, denominational support is a strong predictor of successful fund raising (Dean 1985).

A substantial history of effort in fund raising is also generally related to institutional success. History provides an opportunity for experience and practice: a seasoned staff that knows the institution and has developed a local sense of what does and does not work idiosyncratically with the institution. History can also build a sense of expectation or tradition in fund raising. Many graduates of private liberal arts colleges know from the time of application or freshman orientation that they are expected to become loyal and contributing alumni; the names of previous donors they see on residence halls and science laboratories and attached to scholarships serve as a continuing reminder of this expectation. Students at public community colleges, on the other hand, enter and usually leave the institution without such expectations. The efforts that many institutions now put into student-alumni or senior gift programs are one attempt to build a sense of expectation and tradition.

History also provides an opportunity for programs to mature. Programs of alumni involvement and alumni giving typically take years to include regional alumni clubs or to develop strong reserves of volunteer leadership. Cultivation of nonalumni donors takes time, and deferred giving programs typically need five to six years to begin showing results (Beckett 1973). A history of effort also provides the time to build momentum for larger efforts, such as capital campaigns.

The third general factor used to predict success is the effort or priority an institution gives its fund-raising program. Effort is often measured by the size of the fund-raising staff or budget (McGinnis 1980; Pickett 1977; Woods 1987), and the staff at the most effective institutions may be five to seven times the size of the staff at less effective institutions of similar type (Hornbaker 1986). Larger staffs and larger budgets provide the resources for larger and better research on and records of donors, better personal contact with prospective individual, corporate, and foundation donors, solicitation of a higher percentage of alumni, and stronger programs of institutional promotion (Mack 1983; Webb 1982). A larger staff also provides the support to develop case statements, plans, and programs for fund-raising activities.

An institution's capacity may be thought of as the hypothetical maximum private support an institution could raise under the best conditions.

A commonly used indicator of the priority an institution gives its fund-raising efforts is the relationship of the president to the fund-raising program. While no single best organizational pattern appears overall (McGinnis 1980), at smaller institutions, the direct involvement of the president in making calls on prospective donors has some predictive power for success (Glennon 1985; Steinberg 1984), and at historically black institutions, effective presidential speeches can provide a voice appealing for funds, reinforce common beliefs, and provide impetus for perseverance (Bell 1977). At larger institutions with more fund-raising staff to call on donors, a better organizational indicator seems to be a direct reporting relationship of the chief development officer (CDO) to the president and the involvement of the CDO in institutional planning and setting priorities (Webb 1982).

Taken together, these factors can help explain differences among types of institutions. Newer institutions have smaller pools of alumni and shorter histories of fund raising. Many public colleges have less wealthy student bodies than do private institutions, and the selection and role of trustees in many public institutions almost ensure little active involvement in fund raising. Public institutions without strong traditions of private fund raising or substantial expectations from their states that they will or should raise private support often have difficulty assigning sufficient resources to strengthen fund-raising programs.

Of these three general factors—capacity, history, and effort or priority—capacity is the least amenable to change. Fund raisers or presidents can do little to change the size or wealth of the pool of alumni, and efforts at institutional impact on regional economic success are problematic. History is somewhat amenable to influence, because history continues to create itself; further, institutions can take some effort to build traditions or expectations of private support. For example, it is widely held that a successful campaign raises the level of expectation for continued giving. The effort or priority an institution assigns to its fund raising is the most amenable to the direct influence of presidents, other officers, and governing boards. Beyond indicating that more effort or a higher priority will over time likely produce greater success in fund raising, however, research is of little direct help to specific institutions in assigning newly invested resources in specific programs. Nor does a greater investment address con-

siderations of efficiency and marginal costs. General principles
of management that suggest improved research and record
keeping, planning and setting priorities, matching effort to
strategic advantage and institutional mission, and institutionally based evaluation represent the best available advice.

ORGANIZATION AND COSTS

The only central office was under my hat.
—William Lawrence (1926), working with two colleagues on
a turn-of-the-century fund-raising campaign at Harvard

Two pressing questions from practitioners in fund raising,
particularly newcomers, are what programs to offer and at
what cost. Fund raising is largely motivated by the inadequacies of higher education budgets, and decisions about
starting new programs in fund raising or advancement mindful
of their costs send decision makers looking for advice about
which programs to initiate and what return to expect on their
investment. While the literature does not provide the direct
answers to these questions, some general guidance is
available.

Organization

The organization of fund raising within institutions of higher
education is quite varied. Not only does great variety exist
in the components included in fund raising and where fund
raising is placed in the overall institution; what related components are included with fund raising also vary. The often-
recommended inclusion of admissions, athletics, alumni, com-
munications, capital projects, fund raising, government relations, and public relations under the umbrella of *advancement* may be viewed as the consistent ideal of organization,
but it is rarely an actuality.

The concepts of development and advancement are quite
new in higher education. In the 1950s, two major works on
financing of higher education failed to mention "development," and in 1970, the *Directory of Colleges and Universities*
showed fewer than 25 percent of institutions had such a formal integrated function at the level of vice president or director (Ishoy 1972).

In 1957, the American Alumni Council (AAC) and the American College Public Relations Association (ACPRA) held a joint
conference to focus on coordinating and strengthening their
common efforts. Their report, "The Advancement of Understanding and Support of Higher Education," nicknamed the
"Greenbrier Report," first articulated the principle of consistent and integrated organization of efforts in advancement,
and the two groups later merged to become the Council for
Advancement and Support of Education (CASE).

A clear trend toward greater organization of fund raising and a broader conceptualization of advancement since the Greenbrier Report are evident from surveys of higher education. For example, a 1971 survey of public and private colleges and universities found that more than half had organized fund-raising programs and that almost half of the balance indicated an intention to establish one (Meyer 1971). Most programs were 20 years old or younger, and, predictably, the private colleges had the older and more sophisticated fund-raising efforts—reporting a planned giving office, capital campaign, or other indicators of advanced programming—followed by the private and public universities, with the public colleges bringing up the rear. A survey of land-grant universities some 15 years later reported that three-quarters of institutions reporting had organized offices of advancement—with few of them more than 10 years old—and almost all respondents included alumni relations, fund raising, and public relations within the rubric of "advancement" (Jefferson 1985).

A study of institutional effectiveness in fund raising, using a comprehensive sampling of institutions, reports data on components of organization and practice (Loessin, Duronio, and Borton 1988b). These data are instructive as to what the most common core of programs and practices is in this national, comprehensive sample. Seventy-five percent or more of the respondents reported several practices:

- Setting goals for voluntary support
- Using year-end results for evaluation and setting goals
- Involving the president and fund-raising staff in setting goals
- Automating, at least partially, record keeping
- Using mass mailings and phonathons
- Holding regional alumni events
- Identifying alumni for major gifts
- Soliciting faculty and staff
- Identifying potential donors among nonalumni, foundations, and corporations
- Establishing a matching gifts program.

This list suggests that sound practices and organization have become increasingly more widespread and sophisticated in the past 30 years.

Costs of Fund Raising

The cost of raising a dollar by the Red Cross during World War II was three cents.

Institutional spending is the most consistently reported variable associated with the effectiveness of institutional fund-raising programs. The more sophisticated studies define effectiveness with an adjustment for estimated potential, which is variously defined but usually takes into account internal and external resources available to the institution. An institution with a rich and large alumni body, a location and a research program favorable to corporate and foundation interests, a high regional per capita income, and high productivity among local businesses, for example, would be deemed to have a high potential; one lacking these attributes would be at the low end.

With or without adjustments for estimated potential, the variable representing spending on fund raising seems to be the best correlate of the effectiveness of fund raising, suggesting that an institution wishing to increase its results should consider increasing the amount spent on fund raising. A decision to increase institutional spending should have the benefit of some reasoned assessment of how much more to spend with regard to expected returns. Very little reliable research exists on capacity and effort, or how much an increase in spending will yield in improved results, or the extent to which the results are subject to diminishing returns, however. Little information is available to suggest the necessary or desirable level of spending vis-a-vis the management of marginal costs, although a few extant analyses of spending patterns and fund-raising costs and some excellent reviews of the subject serve as a starting point.

The best known review of institutional spending on advancement and institutional capacity is the work of John W. Leslie, who reviewed American institutions' spending patterns on institutional advancement programs. His review of the variables thought to be significant in the assessment of potential concludes that we are far short of a simple formulation of these variables in assessing institutional capacity or potential for fund raising or setting fund-raising expenditures for optimal results (Leslie 1979). From his work and that of others, one can conclude that the range of dollars spent per dollar raised varies enormously, from a few pennies per dollar raised to half or more of the return (Duronio, Loessin, and Nirschel 1989; Isherwood 1986; Paton 1986; Ramsden 1979; Willmer 1980). The only consistent point is that the more successful and more complex institutions spend more as a percentage of their total budgets, that cost per gift dollar is lower among the institutions raising more dollars, and that private institutions tend to spend more as a share of total budgets and to get a better return on that investment. Whether these patterns can be explained by differences in the institutions' potential or differences in their established histories of commitment to and experience with fund raising—or other factors—cannot be determined.

A review of the costs of fund raising found that differences were so great between different types of institutions and that ranges were so wide within institutional types that the authors recommended that their findings be consulted only to see how costs varied by institutional type, not to look for guidance in evaluating one's own institutional costs (Duronio, Loessin, and Nirschel 1989).

> *Fund raising, too, is subject to the law of diminishing returns—the wider the periphery, the greater the effort, the smaller the gift, and the higher the cost.*
> —Harold H. Seymour

Although institutions have a natural interest in knowing how much they should expect to spend to raise a dollar, the research and advice on this matter is far from conclusive. In mature fund-raising programs, for example, private institutions spend about eight cents to raise a dollar, while public institutions spend 12 cents (Fisher 1989); the same book suggests an average of 14 to 17 cents per dollar (Evans 1989). A study of small colleges found that they spend an average of 14 to 19 cents per dollar (Glennon 1985). One suggestion for mature programs is 15 cents per dollar as the top of the acceptable range of costs (Fisher 1989), while another author suggests 20 to 25 cents per dollar as being high but acceptable (Evans 1989). Yet another author reports that institutions raising between $150,000 and $600,000 can expect to spend 25 to 29 cents to raise a dollar (Willmer 1980).

Costs of fund raising may vary by type of donor or method of solicitation. Reasonable costs for various types of programs are 15 to 35 percent for annual giving, below 10 percent for major gifts, below 10 percent for corporate gifts, and below 5 percent for foundation gifts (Evans 1989). The additional cost of a capital campaign has been estimated at 3 to 10 percent of target (Evans 1989) or 5 to 15 percent (Bornstein 1989a), with small campaigns costing relatively more. The cost of the typical direct mail and phonathon program has been estimated at 30 percent of the amount raised (Wisdom 1989). These cost estimates are not well documented by research, however, and they are likely to vary by type of institution, effort, capacity, and the track record a school has in raising funds from a particular source.

Normative data on total spending, the share it represents of an institution's total expenditures, or the average cost per gift dollar do little to help an institution assess its potential or monitor its efficiency. More promising is the approach using the hypothetical curves of *predisposition* and *capacity* (Paton 1986). These curves serve as a model for determining how closely one is approaching capacity by monitoring the slope and other changes in the curve of return for effort expended. Monitoring *marginal cost*—the increased cost associated with an increase in funds raised—is far more important than average cost in assessing overall performance. Marginal cost probably declines if an institution increases effort when it is far from its potential—and probably rises as the institution grows closer to its maximum potential fund raising. If, for example, an institution makes no effort at fund raising but receives occasional and unsolicited or uncultivated gifts, then its cost per dollar raised is theoretically zero. As efforts are made to cultivate donors and raise funds, the cost per dollar raised for these additional dollars can only rise. An institution with a small or modest fund-raising program but far from its maximum potential can probably raise additional dollars with decreases, or only small increases, in its marginal fund-raising cost; an institution very close to its maximum would experience rather large increases in marginal costs to raise additional dollars. As an institution adds more effort and expense, it approaches its hypothetical maximum, all the time noting increases in marginal costs (or diminishing returns on the investment of effort and expense). When that theoretical ceiling of potential is reached, increased expenditures and efforts will produce no gains whatsoever.

Institutions interested in evaluating their own performance should not rely on average costs compared with other institutions but should monitor changes in marginal costs as a means of estimating their approach to their theoretical maximums (Paton 1986). This advice, combined with the suggested monitoring of allocations to advancement, percent of educational and general budget spent on advancement, and information about gifts by source and purpose, and the near-universal call for more consistent reporting of data about costs, is probably the best approach for an institution attempting to evaluate its costs, efforts, and outcomes.

DONORS' BEHAVIOR AND THEIR MOTIVATION

Gifts can be seen as motivated in part to win favor with the beneficiary, [and] gifts to churches can be seen as buying some influence with the Almighty. Andrew Mellon gave his church money for building a rather magnificent new edifice. A member of the congregation was overheard referring to it as "Andy's Fire Escape."
—Bakal (1981, p. 212)

...determining who is psychologically or emotionally connected to the institution, and why—is essential to the successful marketing of fund-raising efforts

Knowledge of donors' behavior and motivation is critical to the practicing fund raiser. As input to the design of a marketing strategy, it can inform the choice of timing for solicitation and campaigns (economic considerations), the particular pitch (emotional versus collaborative ties), and the size of the request (group and organizational motivation and elasticity). The shift from charity and toward philanthropy of fund raising for higher education in the last hundred years has come about largely as a result of an increased understanding of donors' motivation. Early educational institutions' religious roots suggested that appeals should be charitable, that they should offer the donor the chance to give the disadvantaged the benefits of salvaging sustenance. But today, Stanford University and Miami-Dade Community College are hardly pitiable; a philanthropic rather than charitable pitch characterizes their approach to donors and, in a more comprehensive sense, their model of the relationship between donor and beneficiary.

Modeling Donors' Behavior and Motivation

Two simple but competing explanations of donors' behavior are a charitable model and an economic model. The charitable model assumes that giving is based on altruism, on notions of the advantaged helping the deprived. Econometric models suggest that donations are a function of income, the frequency of messages for the public good, provision of tax incentives, and disincentives to a free ride among nondonors. *The Economy of Love and Fear* (Boulding 1973) advances the notion of grants economics—the economics of one-way transfers of money or goods, such as through taxation, redistribution of income, payments within families (e.g., college tuition for one's children), and charity. The traditional exchange economics cannot adequately explain "grants" (meaning any one-way transfer), but such simplistic economic models as explanations of the behavior of individuals and groups as donors are of limited usefulness (Boulding 1973).

Many additional factors might account for giving that are not accounted for in altruistic or economic models. Private giving may be partly explained by such motives as buying acclaim and friendship, yielding to general egoistic desires, assuaging feelings of guilt, maximizing profits, repaying advantages received (such as college alumni might wish to do), investing in activities that have indirect utility to the donor (such as investment in research and service activities of a college or foundation), or receiving the tangible perquisites of private giving. Because sociologists have somewhat ignored the behavior of giving and studies by psychologists have generally been contrived experiments, empirical studies of giving have been left largely to economists (Jencks 1987).

Economists tend to label philanthropic gifts as "charity," a simplistic and misleading application of the term (Jencks 1987). While "charity" connotes the advantaged helping the deprived, only about 10 percent of philanthropic giving is charitable in the sense employed by economists (Jencks 1987). Combining *charity theory* and *exchange theory* accounts for giving by individuals or corporations (Drachman 1983). The economists' exchange theory is based on a two-person, two-good situation in which each party benefits from the mutual exchange of tangible goods. The part about tangible goods was a stumbling block in developing theories of private giving until economists decided that charity theory could be based upon the utility to the donor of the gift given. The utility could be altruism or an indirect benefit (maintaining or enhancing the prestige of one's alma mater) or more direct (the prestige associated with giving).

Based on a review of recent empirical findings, one author challenges the classic notions of donors' altruism, the assumption in economics of a direct relationship between giving and tax, income distribution, and size of population (Andreoni 1986). The findings also fail to support the Samuelsonian notion of a free ride among nondonors and the notion that public provision drives out private philanthropy. The preferred model includes the notion of "impure altruism," in which the donor enjoys additional utility beyond altruism from the act of giving.

Economic models of the exchanges of gifts differ from exchanges in the marketplace in several ways, the most obvious being that in market exchanges, money (or goods) is exchanged for goods or services and a sense of balance and completeness is achieved; that is, the transaction is completed. In exchanges of gifts, a gift upsets the balance and the recipient is beholden to the giver, calling for another exchange in which the donor and recipient change places. Applied to education, gift exchange theory suggests that the college gave its alumni their advantage in life, their education, and their first jobs—all substantial gifts. It then asks the grateful alumni to give to annual and capital campaigns—to give time, energy, leadership, and emotional support. The college responds with its return gifts of recognition and its announced perquisites of membership in giving clubs, luncheons, honorary plaques, tokens and invitations to briefings and dedications, honorary degrees, and even the donor's name on a building. In response to these gifts—their return on earlier gifts—donors are cultivated to even higher levels of giving and receive even higher levels of gifts in exchange. The cycle ratchets ever higher.

Developing models of donors' behavior—understanding donors' motivations, determining who is psychologically or emotionally connected to the institution and why—is essential to the successful marketing of fund-raising efforts, from individuals, such as alumni, to businesses and other organizations to corporations and foundations with formal charitable mechanisms and goals to trustees and fellow employees. Often research about donors' behavior is couched in alumni surveys of status and attitude. Alumni research is often specific to an institution and not "clean enough" to add to the general storehouse of knowledge (Melchiori *in press* a). Research done within institutions generally has the purpose of increasing donations from alumni, and questions in surveys are worded so they do not offend any alumni; consequently, they seldom ask what we really need to know.

An Overview of Donors' Behavior

> *Tinsel doesn't attract gold.*
> —John A. Pollard

Studies of general giving behavior, some of which draw upon large-scale data banks, can provide some useful insights for higher education. While giving increases with age (Jencks

1987), little evidence suggests whether the statement is true for all cohorts or whether people born in the late 19th and early 20th centuries have simply given more all of their lives. The evidence also indicates that people who are married or widowed give more than single people and that people with dependent children give more than others, even when income level and tax bracket are held constant. "These findings suggest that concern for others is not usually a zero sum sentiment in which family members 'use up' their concern for others on one another and have nothing 'left over' for outsiders. Instead, our concern for others seems to expand when we live with others" (Jencks 1987, p. 327). Reversing the direction in that inference might also lead one to conclude that people with more concern for others are more likely to marry, raise children, and maintain intact family households.

Further analysis of demographic data tends to confirm, though not conclusively, the general belief that women are more generous and suggests that Protestants may give more than Catholics. More important to higher education, estimates indicate that an extra year's schooling adds 5 percent in charitable giving, holding income constant (Jencks 1987), and that people who give $500 or more per year make larger average gifts to higher education than to any other type of organization (Hodgkinson and Weitzman 1986).

Research on private giving suggests that motivations for and patterns of giving differ significantly by the circumstances of the donor and the target of the gifts; the circumstances and motivations for giving to religion, education, charity, and the arts differ in significant ways. Overall studies of private giving reveal a U-shaped curve, with the largest giving, as a percent of income, among the least and the most affluent.

Wealthy respondents tend to give higher proportions of their total charitable gifts to colleges and universities than do less wealthy respondents, whose giving tends to favor religion (Balz 1987). Donors to private colleges and universities are more likely to be giving to additional colleges and universities than are donors to public institutions. Among donors to private institutions, giving to colleges and universities is a higher percent of total charitable giving. Public institutions obtain about two-thirds of their total private giving from gifts over $5,000, private institutions more than three-quarters.

In a study of major donors, the author interviewed 30 donors of $1 million or more, asking them to tell what motivated them to make such gifts (Hunter 1975). Their primary responses were worthiness of the cause, personal interest or association with the cause, knowledge that the organization was managed well, a sense of real social need, a sense of community obligation, and tax benefits.

Correlational analyses from a survey of over 300 institutions give clues to varying motivations by type of donor (Loessin, Duronio, and Borton 1988b). Alumni giving appears independent of the institution's tuition, number of alumni of record, and type of institution, suggesting that successful alumni giving programs are now conducted in all types and sizes of institutions. The association between alumni giving and expenditures for fund raising, on the other hand, suggests that alumni giving is related to regular reminders and encouragements to give. Giving among nonalumni is associated with the size of the institutional budget and the market value of the endowment, suggesting that these donors are influenced by prestige-related variables and a tradition of private support at the institution.

Giving by corporate donors is associated with the size of the institutional budget, the number of alumni of record, and the institution's expenditures for fund raising, which can be interpreted as reflections of the importance corporate donors place on the "capacity to perform" and may be related to the institution's size and research mission (Loessin, Duronio, and Borton 1988b). Foundations' giving is correlated with a college's or university's expenditures for fund raising, the value of its endowment, expenditures per student, and the total size of its budget. These relationships suggest that foundations' giving is related to the success an institution has with other donors and its overall wealth.

Table 4 shows predictors of voluntary support, by type of donor, for 73 Carnegie-classified Research Universities (I) (Leslie and Ramey 1988). Although some variables affect all groups of donors similarly, some affect groups of donors differently and to very different degrees. *Size* was consistently significant as a predictor of giving, but this factor should be interpreted as local and regional impact; larger institutions are more influential in their locales than are smaller institutions (Leslie and Ramey 1988). *Spending per student* was positively related to giving among nonalumni individuals and foundations, suggesting that these donors believe in a relationship between price and quality. Alumni may respond to emphasis on traditions and prestige—age of institution and quality rating—and both groups of individuals may respond favorably to shortfalls in state appropriations. Business donations are higher to institutions located in areas of economic growth.

TABLE 4

PREDICTORS OF GIVING: RESEARCH UNIVERSITIES

	Individuals		Organizations		Total
	Alumni	*Nonalumni*	*Business*	*Nonbusiness*	
Measures of quality					
Quality rating					
Age of institution	+				
Expenditure per student		+		+	+
Fund-raising Effort					
Percent solicited		–			–
Fund-raising history					
Endowment per alumnus		+	+	+	+
State appropriation per FTE Student (public institutions)	–	–			
Regional Economic Growth	+		+		+
Size	+	+	+	+	+
R2	.56	.60	.46	.45	.71

Source: Leslie and Ramey 1988.

A limited number of studies has also been conducted on distinctive types of institutions. Alumnae of women's colleges, for example, have been shown to be nearly twice as likely to be donors as are graduates of coed institutions. The Women's College Coalition (1988) compared data from 354 private coed colleges to 51 four-year private women's colleges and found that the average gift by an alumna of a women's college is 26 percent larger than that of graduates of coed colleges in their sample. For the decade ending in 1987, women's colleges showed greater gains than coed colleges in a range of types of private support: average gift, total giving, realized bequests, the share of unrestricted gifts, and corporate matched gifts. These changes may be attributed to a high degree of loyalty, increased earnings and greater financial sophistication among alumnae, increased control over discretionary income, and more effective fund-raising practices among the women's colleges.

Alumni giving to historically black colleges and universities has been quite limited, although current efforts are under way to build expectations and traditions of giving to such institutions. Evidence suggests that alumni of historically black colleges have more positive attitudes toward giving if the college president is perceived to be an effective writer and speaker, if the public image of the institution is high, and if the alumni give positive ratings to the quality and quantity of alumni correspondence, the quality of alumni programs, and to their experiences as undergraduate students (Evans 1986).

Predicting Alumni Giving

A national survey of previous college students indicates that about one-quarter of people who have attended college have donated at some time to their undergraduate institution; one-quarter who have not donated indicate they have not been asked (Lindenmann 1983). Donations were higher among those who have earned a baccalaureate (40 percent) than among those who did not (13.5 percent); most likely from those who had attended a religious college (48 percent), followed by an independent college (33 percent) and a public institution (22 percent); slightly more likely from women (28 percent) than from men (24 percent); and increasingly likely as level of income increased (20 percent of those earning less than $15,000 gave, compared to 52 percent of those making over $40,000). Loyalty to one's alma mater was an important factor in giving, cited more often by those who had attended independent schools (76 percent) than public institutions (57 percent).

A relatively large number of surveys predicts alumni donors or classifies them at various levels of giving. Most of the studies are dissertations, and most are based on a single institution, most often a university. The results, summarized in table 5, do not support strong conclusions. In general, characteristics or behaviors of alumni while they were students are not strong predictors of future giving; no conclusive pattern supports differences based on entering ability, patterns of attendance, participation in student organizations, place of residence, choice of major, or grade point average. Findings on financial aid are mixed, with some suggestion that likely predictors of giving are either receiving no financial aid or receiving scholarships (as opposed to loans). It may be the case that students who do not feel economically disadvantaged by the costs of college attendance are more likely to become alumni donors.

The findings on the current status, beliefs, and behavior of alumni are somewhat more helpful in predicting their behavior as donors, though simple demographic variables prove poor predictors. Age, sex, marital status, and having children are poor predictors, but some evidence indicates that the relationship between age and giving is curvilinear, with the largest donations coming from age groups in the middle of the distribution. This phenomenon represents the crossing of two curves: *motivation* (a diminution of alumni motivation as their time distance from the institution increases) and *capacity* (as they earn more they can afford to give more) (Connolly and Blanchette 1986).

Earning one or more degrees from an institution is a consistent predictor of giving. Occupation is not a consistent predictor, although some evidence suggests that alumni in higher-paying fields may be more likely to give or to give more.

Perhaps the best predictors of alumni giving are an emotional attachment to the school, participation in alumni events, and participation in and donation to other voluntary and religious groups. While these variables are the most consistently reported indicators of alumni giving and can be fairly easily measured through survey research, they are not those most likely to be contained in an alumni data base and their utility in selecting alumni likely to give or give more is thus limited.

Tax Incentives, Economics, and Donors' Behavior

The top 1 percent of taxpayers make 15 percent of total charitable contributions and 36 percent of all gifts of property.
—The Internal Revenue Service

One principal component of the cost of charity is the deductibility of charitable gifts. Federal income tax dates back to 1913. Individuals have been allowed to deduct charitable contributions since 1917; corporations have been permitted to do so since 1935. It is reasonable to believe that philanthropy will rise if more money is available and decline when less

TABLE 5

PREDICTIONS OF ALUMNI DONATIONS

Variables	Predictors	Nonpredictors
Information from Student Years		
Distance to school at time of admission	McKee (1975)	
Higher SAT or ACT score	Dahl (1981)	Korvas (1984)
Entry as freshman or transfer		Korvas (1984)
Attended all four years	Gardner (1975)	
Age (23+) at time of admission	Korvas (1984)	
Participation in student groups	Keller (1982)	McNally (1985)
	Haddad (1986)	Beeler (1982)
	Gardner (1975)	Korvas (1984)
Mortar Board (for student activities)	Dietz (1985)	
Place of residence while in school		Korvas (1984)
		Haddad (1986)
		Dietz (1985)
Greek affiliate	Haddad (1986)	Dietz (1985)
Received financial aid	Beeler (1982)	Korvas (1984)
		Haddad (1986)
Thought it was sufficient	Korvas (1984)	
Lower for loan recipients	Dietz (1985)	
Amount of college costs borrowed		Korvas (1984)
Academic performance		Beeler (1982)
		Korvas (1984)
Full- or part-time studies		Korvas (1984)
Day students give more	Korvas (1984)	
Years of attendance		
Those with more years give less	Korvas (1984)	
Academic major		Korvas (1984)
		Keller (1982)
		McNally (1985)
Arts and sciences give more than		
management	Beeler (1982)	
Liberal arts and sciences	Haddad (1986)	
Engineering	Dietz (1985)	
Obtained job through placement		Haddad (1986)
Current information		
Sex		McKee (1975)
		Korvas (1984)
		Keller (1982)
Men give more	Haddad (1986)	
	McNally (1985)	
Marital status		Beeler (1982)
		Korvas (1984)
		Keller (1982)
Married	Dietz (1985)	
Spouse attended/is also an alumna		Korvas (1984)
		Keller (1982)

Variables	Predictors	Nonpredictors
Spouse contributed to college	Haddad (1986)	
Status of children		
Have children		Beeler (1982)
		Korvas (1984)
Two children	Haddad (1986)	
Children currently in college		Korvas (1984)
Children 18 or older	Haddad (1986)	
Current distance to school		Korvas (1984)
		Keller (1982)
		Haddad (1986)
Closer	McKee (1975)	
Farther	Beeler (1982)	
Degrees earned		McNally (1985)
Undergraduate degree	McKee (1975)	
	Dahl (1981)	
More than one degree	McKee (1975)	
Graduate education	Beeler (1982)	Korvas (1984)
Occupation		McNally (1985)
		Keller (1982)
Education-related	McKee (1975)	
Managerial and professional	Beeler (1982)	
Life science–related	Dietz (1985)	
Income		
Over $10,000	Korvas (1984)	
Over $15,000	Dietz (1985)	
Alumni programs		
Participation	McKee (1975)	
	Korvas (1984)	
	Keller (1982)	
	Haddad (1986)	
Reads alumni publications	Kelly (1979)	
Number of years as dues payer	Kelly (1979)	
Satisfaction with alumni events		Korvas (1984)
Visits to college per year		Korvas (1984)
Maintains close contact	Carlson (1978)	
Current knowledge of school		Korvas (1984)
Age		McNally (1985)
		Korvas (1984)
Older give more	Haddad (1986)	
Middle group gives most	McKee (1975)	
Emotional attachment to school	McKee (1975)	
	Beeler (1982)	
	Gardner (1975)	
	Carlson (1978)	
Religion		
Practicing member of a group	Kelly (1979)	
Active in church of school affiliation	Gardner (1975)	
Other behavior		
Gives to other causes	Markoff (1978)	
Participates in voluntary organizations	Markoff (1978)	

Variables	Predictors	Nonpredictors
Belongs to special-interest groups	McNally (1985)	
Gives to graduate alma mater		Korvas (1984)
Beliefs		
Alumni and friends should give	MacIsaac (1973)	
President should raise funds	MacIsaac (1973)	
Tax incentives spur gifts	MacIsaac (1973)	
No contact explains no gifts	MacIsaac (1973)	
School had positive influence	Korvas (1984)	
School quality currently high	Korvas (1984)	
Positive feelings about school	McKinney (1978)	
Politically conservative (as is school)	Gardner (1975)	

is available, that private giving will increase if the cost of giving is lower and decrease if the cost of giving rises. The two most recent tests of this notion were the tax reforms of 1986 and the stock market crash of late 1987. As those who did not expect to itemize in the future made their last deductible gifts, a rush of private giving to higher education was experienced in late 1986, swelling slightly the 1986 reports of giving. After private voluntary support for higher education posted 15 consecutive years of 12 percent average annual gains, 1987–88 faltered but apparently because of the rush in late 1986 and some conservatism resulting from the market meltdown in the fall of 1987. The other consequence of tax reform, the increased cost of charity (those in the top bracket are paying 67 cents for a one dollar gift now, up from 50 cents before 1987), seems to have influenced giving to higher education, with a reduction of 3.5 percent over 1986–87. Gifts most susceptible to the influence of such reform—appreciated gifts and gifts over $5,000—were particularly affected (Bailey 1989, p. 8).

The market crash of 1987 reduced the dollar value of most endowments significantly, but income from those endowments—the immediate concern of college administrators—was not much affected. Furthermore, several institutions launching campaigns—MIT's $550 million campaign, for example—reported that progress was undiminished in any detectable way by the events of October 1987. While it is tempting to interpret these gross data and anecdotes, the research on the influence of tax incentives, cost of giving, and economic factors is more illuminating.

An examination of economic trends related to giving trends over time, using a time series analysis on total giving to higher education for 1932 to 1974, concludes that businesses tended to adjust giving to the current economic climate, while individuals—alumni and nonalumni—gave without regard to, or even despite, economic conditions (Drachman 1983). The implications for fund-raising strategy are that different characteristics should be stressed when dealing with different donors. Alumni and nonalumni should be solicited in different ways; businesses and individuals should be pursued at different times and with different approaches with regard to economic conditions and the demonstrated needs of the institution.

Several studies conducted on the effect on donors of the deductibility of charitable contributions show that the incentive of deductibility is higher among individuals receiving higher incomes; that is, donations are inversely related to price and directly related to income (Schwartz 1970; Taussig 1967). Gifts to education and hospitals appear particularly price sensitive; eliminating deductibility would appear to cut giving to educational institutions and hospitals by half although leaving religion largely unaffected (Feldstein 1975).

A U-shaped distribution of charitable giving is related to family income, with the tipping point about twice the median family income (when charitable contributions as a percent of income begin to rise again) (Jencks 1987). For example, 1981 IRS data on taxpayers who itemize (who give more than taxpayers who do not) show that as a percent of adjusted gross income (AGI), taxpayers with incomes under $10,000 gave about 6.2 percent; the low point, 2.3 percent, was for taxpayers with AGIs from $25,000 to $49,999, after which giving rises again to 4.1 percent in the $100,000 to $499,999 bracket and to 8.9 percent among those reporting AGIs of $500,000 or more. The tentative explanation is that individuals have two motives for giving: *paying your dues* and *giving away your surplus* (Jencks 1987). Giving to churches is paying your dues; as income rises, giving to churches increases, but not proportionately. Giving to colleges (and hospitals) is more like giving away your surplus. Much alumni giving is to major private institutions, whose graduates tend to do well economically, and much of the total giving to higher education is from nonalumni who give for such purposes as buildings and endowed chairs. The U-shaped distribution of giving with respect to income is a product of these two motives at work. With regard to tax incentives, the rich are understandably more sensitive to taxes, but the relationship is more with marginal tax rate than with absolute level of income (Jencks 1987).

Donors' Behavior and Intercollegiate Athletics

I would rather see the color of the blue-tipped oars first across the finish line than gaze at the matchless splendor of a masterpiece of Titian. I would rather watch the hats go over the across bar after a Yale victory than the finest dramatic performance the world has ever known. I would rather hear "March, March on Down the Field" rather than listen to the music of a great opera (Rudolph 1962, p. 430).
—An alumni speaker at the victory celebration at the New York Yale club honoring the crew team that had defeated Harvard in 1922

One controversial aspect of donors' behavior is the effect of athletic teams' success on giving. Some argue that success in athletics brings favorable attention and recognition to a college or university, increases pride and bonding among alumni, and has a positive spillover effect on all fund raising at the institution. Others argue that athletic success motivates only a small proportion of alumni and can have the effect of diminishing the academic reputation of a college enjoying athletic success and thus have neutral or deleterious effects on private support. The question has been around and studied longer than almost any other research question in fund raising for higher education.

We are told that alumni contributions are important. Well, I have watched alumni, and my observation is that alumni are all talk and no money. The largest hot-air balloon that floats over the average university is the myth about alumni giving. If you need a new stadium, the alumni run around foaming at the mouth, promising you the sky if you build it, but giving you nothing. Alumni are good at threatening you with reprisals, but they don't even give you a chance to watch their checks bounce. Pleasing the alumni is the big excuse for having intercollegiate football, but it is not legitimate (Mitchell 1982, pp. 22–24).

One of the best-documented inquiries in the history of fund raising is of the widely held conviction that winning teams produce higher yields in private giving, often bolstered only

One of the best-documented inquiries in the history of fund raising is of the widely held conviction that winning teams produce higher yields in private giving

by anecdotes of institutions where winning teams appeared to induce increased private giving or losing teams to reduce it. Few areas of inquiry into fund raising have been as long and as thoroughly examined, yet few areas of conventional thinking and practice in higher education seem so clearly at odds with the empirical findings.

As many as 70 years ago, Dr. Arnaud Marts, president of Bucknell, reviewed the fortunes of 16 colleges emphasizing football and 16 comparable schools that did not from 1921 to 1923. The endowments of the nonfootball schools outgrew those of the football schools (1934). He observed that many colleges thought investments in football would be of value in attracting students and gift dollars, yet his findings were clearly at odds with any positive causal link. While the methodology is flawed, the findings were a portent of almost all research on this subject since. A study of 151 institutions that dropped football between 1939 and 1974, for example, concludes that the schools experienced no significant negative effects from dropping football and that some institutions actually experienced significantly positive results (Springer 1974).

While some of the writing about athletics and giving is largely anecdotal—a lengthy list of individual cases documents where winning teams seemed to spark increased giving, for example (Amdur 1971)—much sophisticated methodology, design, and analysis have been applied to this area of inquiry. Some researchers have defined athletic success as percent of winning season, bowl invitations, and conference ranking and successful fund raising as annual giving, annual giving by alumni, total giving, and increases adjusted for economic conditions. They have separated analyses by geographic area, athletic conference, sport, level, and availability of other local spectator sports and have looked one, three, five, and ten years after athletic success for influence on giving. Despite this sophistication, little variation occurs in the findings (see table 6). Over a considerable variety of methodologies and samples, numerous studies display remarkably similar results: Nothing suggests a positive relationship between total giving and athletic success, and only scant evidence suggests that in some types of institutions, within a narrow definition of giving and within some donor groups, some association exists.

While ample evidence suggests that the presence of an emotional tie to one's college is related to making a donation as a graduate and one form of that emotional tie is reflected

TABLE 6

EFFECTS OF ATHLETIC SUCCESS ON FUND RAISING

Study	Effect[a]	Notes
Cutlip (1965)	0/some −	
Spaeth and Greeley (1970)		Football only/private
Budig (1976)	0/−	Football (0)/Basketball (−)
Sigelman and Carter (1979)	0/some −	
Brooker and Klastorin (1981)	0/some +	Private/church-related only
Sigelman and Bookheimer (1983)	0/some +	Athletic giving only
Gaski and Etzel (1984)	0	
Frederick (1984)	−	Football/some + outcomes with less successful teams

[a] 0 = no effect; − = negative; + = positive.

in athletics, both sophisticated and unsophisticated methods demonstrate very little link between athletic success and alumni giving. The search for evidence will no doubt continue as long as intuition suggests that the link *must* exist. Yet almost nowhere else in the research literature on fund raising in higher education is the research more thorough and rigorous, more plentiful, or more convincing. A handful of anecdotes seems to outweigh the carefully conducted serious research in dictating what is known about athletics and donors' behavior. (As an interesting contrast to the rather one-directional conclusion of this review, one might want to read the views of the athletic boosters, fund raisers, and public relations staffs reflected in the writing provided in the more journalistic summaries by Frey [1985] or Lederman [1988].)

Corporations' and Foundations' Behavior as Donors

The fostering of higher education in America by the modern business corporation [is] as new and strange as the adventure of the duck [that] adopted the kitten (Allem 1968, p. iv).

American corporations have long understood the value and importance of private voluntary support of higher education. The General Electric Company pioneered in corporate giving to higher education by providing equipment grants in the early 1900s. DuPont gave gifts to support higher education during World War I, and both Sears and Westinghouse supported higher education financially as early as the 1930s. Corporate donations to higher education increased from $38 million in 1940 to $70 million in 1953.

Financial support for higher education from corporations before the 1950s almost always came in the form of financial aid to employees or their families. In 1951, the Ford Motor Company announced 70 scholarships for children of employees to include, in addition to tuition and students' expenses, $500 to the *private* college or university the student chose—a "cost of education supplement" as it came to be called (Allem 1968).

In 1952 Union Carbide and Carbon announced a scholarship program not restricted to company employees, and in 1955 General Electric began the "Corporate Alumnus Program," which marked the beginning of matching gift programs, in part to help direct support to the colleges that actually educated its employees and to help express gratitude for that education.

A court decision in 1953 allowing corporate donations to higher education further reduced the reluctance and removed the legal obstacle to corporations' giving to higher education, making way for the tremendous gains in corporate giving in the next three decades.

Corporations

Among the estimated million and a half corporations in America, fewer than 25 percent of them make charitable contributions, and only 7.5 percent give more than $500 per year. Support for higher education today represents 35 percent of corporations' budgets for contributions in the United States—and more than 50 percent for many companies. Corporate support of higher education, which stood at $38 million in 1940, grew from $70 million to $700 million between 1953 and 1978 (Council for Financial 1979). By 1987–88, an estimated $1.85 billion, 22.6 percent of total private voluntary support to higher education, was given by corporations (Council for Aid 1989, p. 3). Considerable evidence suggests that the potential is far from realized, however. Large firms typically give less than 1 percent of their pretax income to charity, and lacking better data about a particular company, this figure is the best indicator of probable giving by a corporation (Useem 1987). In 1981, when the IRS's maximum deductible rate for corporations was first increased from 5 percent to 10 percent of pretax profits, only 10 percent of the firms that gave were at or above the 5 percent level.

Higher education and business are basically interdependent.
One needs money to produce educated people, and the other
needs educated people to produce money.
—Milton Eisenhower, president of Johns Hopkins University,
cited in Council for Financial 1979, p. 6.

Most professional fund raisers and corporate relations officers agree that an important ingredient for success in corporate fund raising is the possible service of the corporation's
self-interest—however remote or convoluted—in the program
or institution asking for the gift. By way of circumspect evidence of this factor of self-interest, several studies have shown
a correlation between corporations' budgets for giving and
for advertising. Whatever the evidence, it is deductively clear
that it is in corporations' interest to give money to higher education for several reasons and causes:

• Education's role in producing trained people as better
  workers in the business community;
• Its basic research, which best flourishes at the university;
• Its public service to support and enrich community life
  (e.g., day care, assistance for small businesses, cultural
  events); and
• Its production of educated people so essential to maintenance of the quality of life.

Some corporate giving can be seen as maintenance of the
morale and quality of life of the corporation's staff. About 8
percent of corporate giving to higher education is to match
the gifts of its own employees, which amounted to almost
$129 million in 1987–88 (Council for Aid 1989, p. 8). Almost
7 percent of the matched amount is in student financial aid
at colleges and universities, both of which may be seen by
employees—or characterized by management—as "fringe
benefits" to employment. Higher education gains from this
source of support as well, as it needs diverse sources of funding to remain free from undue governmental control and to
carry out its essential mission in an atmosphere of freedom.
This exchange is very much analogous to the illustrations of
gift exchange theories of individual donation, where giving
the gift is two-directional and the donor receives something
tangible or intangible from the exchange.

The improvement of the quality of life, however, is not something a corporation can capture exclusively for itself. These improvements pay benefits to all citizens and corporations in the city or region, including the corporations that do not participate in public giving. Consequently, a great deal of peer influence is apparent among corporations within a given community, with levels of giving reflecting general rather than specific corporate support. This influence helps explain the enormous differences in levels of giving among major cities (Useem 1987).

One recent change in federal policy has been described as a reduction in public tax support for public programs with the expectation of a corresponding increase in private voluntary support. Cuts in federal spending begun in 1981 amount to a 20 percent reduction of government support of higher education, $115 billion in a four-year period. With total giving of $3 billion, however, American corporations cannot begin to make up the difference. A 1981 survey of 400 major firms shows that only 6 percent indicated they would increase their giving programs in response to federal cuts.

The Council for Aid to Education recommends that businesses interested in giving to education develop a philosophy, policy, plan, and program to do so, including goals for giving, and suggests that a related charitable foundation can give stability to the corporate support program as the sponsoring corporation wends its way through volatile business and economic cycles (Council for Financial 1979). By 1980, over 80 percent of the top 500 U.S. corporations had a public affairs office, and three-quarters of them were headed by someone with the title "vice president." About half of the almost 800 large firms surveyed in 1981 had a company foundation, with donations from foundations accounting for about 40 percent of all corporate giving (Useem 1987).

Foundations

Approximately 23,600 foundations are active in the United States with total assets of $64.5 billion, or roughly half the total assets of the country's 400 wealthiest people. These foundations award annual grants of $4.8 billion and engage 6,000 employees. According to the 1985 Foundation Directory, 4,402 foundations had assets over $1 million or annual giving over $100,000. This group, representing 18.7 percent of all foundations, held 97 percent of all foundation assets, 85 percent of total grants, and virtually all of the paid staff.

Within that group, 96 foundations, each with assets over $100 million, made 35.8 percent of all grants. Only 15 foundations, with assets of $500 million or more, accounted for approximately 28 percent of all assets, 13.6 percent of total grants, and the majority of paid staff. About 20 percent of the assets of Directory foundations were in New York, and over half of the assets were in the Middle Atlantic or East North Central region.

Foundations' support for higher education in 1986 was approximately 19.6 percent (or $1.6 billion) of total private support for higher education, behind individual sources at 48.4 percent ($4.96 billion) and corporations at 22.6 percent ($1.85 billion).

Although foundations have been credited with a range of innovations in higher education ranging from faculty pensions to honors programs, foundations generally maintain an individually narrow scope of interest. The range of program funding for a foundation is usually defined in its charter (if independent) or by its parent company's interests (in the case of company-sponsored foundations) or geographically (if a public or community foundation). As a result, foundations' influence tends to be maximized by the focus of their interests. Essentially narrow and conservative, working with small staffs and voluntary boards, foundations are necessarily wary of taking risks and trying new ventures: *"In the aggregate,* foundation giving has favored the *more established* agencies, *conventional* fields of interest and modes of operation, and *more advantaged* constituencies"* (Ylvisaker 1987, p. 374).

Studies of Corporations and Foundations as Donors
It appears that corporations respond to requests that can best be turned to the corporation's own interests, either directly or indirectly (Allem 1968; Whitehead 1976). Direct benefits to the corporation, related to maximizing profits, include support for research that advances the company's work and support for the education and training of prospective employees. Indirect benefits include enhancing the image of business in the community (such as through sponsorships), improving employees' morale (such as through matching gift programs and scholarships for employees), and enacting a sense of corporate social responsibility (such as through the enhancement

of the community where the corporation feels it has a stake). This consideration for quality of life provides an environment that is attractive to new employees and rewarding to continuing ones. Corporate support can also be motivated by the desire to maintain a climate conducive to the maintenance of free enterprise.

When asked what common criteria are applied in awarding private gifts, corporate public affairs officers tend to answer the quality of the proposal, the organization's effectiveness and general reputation, and the likelihood of success (Lawson 1976). Yet the only consistent factor from statistical analyses of corporate giving point toward corporate self-interest, including gifts to research universities to advance knowledge of value to the corporation, gifts to the community to enhance the political influence of the business, and the public relations value of giving.

Many corporations that do make donations to higher education have no well-defined set of policies or processes (Callaghan 1975), nor do most have much evidence of the effectiveness of their grants (Useem 1987). Instead, many look toward the advantages of association with large organizations and prestigious institutions. Institutions may increase their success in raising corporate funds by a factor of four to five if their governing boards are populated by well-connected company managers and if they are located near corporate headquarters (Useem 1987).

Institutions may do well to approach potential corporate donors as investors rather than as donors. Approaches can be strengthened with a knowledge of the corporation's past record of giving to higher education, the educational and professional background of corporate personnel, and knowledge of the corporation's policy on giving (Buck 1976). Institutions should also be aware of their own current and potential ties with a particular business through placement services, alumni employees, and—particularly in the case of local corporations—student internships and faculty consulting.

Two-year colleges, whose traditional share of corporate support has been quite low, enroll half of all college students today. Doctoral and comprehensive institutions received 78 percent of corporate support in 1987–88, general baccalaureate and specialized colleges almost 21 percent, and two-year colleges less than 1 percent (Council for Aid 1989, p. 5). The trend for corporate giving to two-year institutions appears to be increasing, however, particularly with corporations' permitting their employees' gifts to two-year colleges to be matched. Despite the widely held belief that companies do not fund two-year colleges because they perceive that they are well (or fully) funded with tax dollars, research does not support a general corporate unwillingness to give to public community colleges (Pokrass 1988). Companies that do support two-year institutions cite as reasons that the colleges are integral parts of the community, that they provide the companies with new employees and with training programs, and that they serve the employees' children. Techniques that can increase corporate support for two-year colleges include advisory committees with corporate members included, consultation with corporations about their training needs, keeping corporations informed of needs for equipment, and paying attention to person-to-person contact with corporate officers (Callahan and Steele 1984). Successful community colleges get to know the companies in their area and make sure the companies know their needs.

Foundations are most likely to support proposals from research universities (37 percent of total dollars in 1974 for a representative group of the largest foundations), least likely to support two-year colleges (1 percent of total dollars), and about twice as likely to support a private as a public institution (Cheit and Lobman 1979). Foundations appear to have conservative interests, tending to be much more narrowly focused, sometimes to the point of supporting only one enterprise or issue, and tending to follow the lead of other, larger foundations. Foundations have been criticized for a relatively low level of support for women's and minority issues, but historically black colleges that involved alumni, faculty, and trustees in fund raising and employed a fund-raising staff were more likely to gain significant support from private foundations (Cheatham 1975).

Foundations are most likely to support proposals from institutions that (1) are located in the same state or (2) the same region, (3) request unrestricted funds, (4) have past experience with foundations, (5) demonstrate sound fiscal management, (6) engender confidence in the institution's president and (7) in the school's administration, and (8) inspire confidence in the school's reputation for academic excellence (Lawson 1976). Because foundations tend to have small staffs, this tendency to follow others may be based on the conviction that if another foundation has found the cause worthy, a lot of staff time in investigation and evaluation can be saved.

CONSIDERATIONS OF ETHICS AND VALUES IN FUND RAISING

Hark! Hark! The dogs do bark,
The beggars are coming to town;
Some in rags, some in tags,
And some in velvet gowns.
—Mother Goose Rhyme

Collectively, gifts for specific purposes can have a major influence on an institution's shape and direction.

How should an institution's values be reflected in its fund-raising program? What ethical considerations do institutions and their chief officers face in raising private support? How do fund raisers balance considerations of the bottom line with personal and institutional values like honesty, trust, openness, and equity in seeking private support? The pressures for institutions to divest themselves of investment holdings with companies doing business in South Africa illustrate how heated the ethical issues related to private support can become on campus.

While some recent cases receiving widespread publicity have highlighted the more dramatic considerations of values and ethics in fund raising, in most instances the issues are played out privately, often with little formal consideration within the institution. The publicized issues illustrate some of the fundamental questions. While Wheaton College, for example, raised money in a major capital campaign, its officers and board members were discussing whether to change the institution from a women's college to a coeducational institution. Following the announced decision to become coeducational, the institution found itself in court, seeking a legal solution to a direct question: What obligation did the institution have to alumnae who believed that their donations were being made to support a women's college? Offering to return donations to disgruntled donors provided a practical solution (*Chronicle* 1988), and the fact that so few accepted the offer may provide some comfort. Nevertheless, the case illustrates difficult questions.

How can officers and trustees balance their need for reasonable confidentiality as they consider a fundamental change in the nature of the institution—for what they believe are reasons of long-term fiscal health—with the importance of maintaining relationships of trust with important friends and supporters of the institution? Using the case of Wheaton College as an illustration, when was the institution obliged to inform donors or potential donors of the consideration of coeducation? Was it obliged to inform some donors earlier than others? If so, which ones? Large donors? Frequent donors? Elected representatives?

For another example, Villanova University accepted a gift of $50,000 in 1985 from a wealthy individual (who had given over $2 million in 20 years) to help retain a successful basketball coach. In 1986, the individual gave over $400,000, and the president did not refuse his offer of an unwanted gift: a Division I wrestling team, coached by the donor. Because the institution had no appropriate facilities, the team operated out of the donor's house, and the donor hired assistant coaches, paying them $1 per year, with supplements of $20,000 to $30,000 to their tax-free Olympic trust funds. The then-president eliminated the wrestling team in 1988 but only after several unsavory events: The local high school team was suspended for a year for practicing out of season with the college team, members of the coaching staff admitted they took student wrestlers out drinking, physical fights broke out between assistant coaches, and a $555,000 lawsuit was filed against the donor and the institution (*Providence Journal-Bulletin* 1988). This case presents an extreme example of issues that often present themselves with more subtlety: To what extent do large gifts, frequent gifts, or timely donations that accomplish a specific purpose create special obligations for an institution toward the donor? What are the nature and the degree of the obligation? When should a gift be refused?

While such highly publicized cases may generate discussion, few avenues are available for organized exploration of fundamental questions. While the literature on fund raising is abundant, "it is a practical literature, written largely by practitioners. It rarely asks questions that might stir doubts or second thoughts in the minds of those it is intended to persuade" (Payton 1988b, p. 63). And while presidents and seasoned fund raisers can easily identify fundamental and recurring dilemmas concerning values and ethics in their work, professional education generally available to them has seldom provided substantial opportunities to explore these difficult issues (Council for Advancement 1985).

These issues of educational fund raising can be categorized into five areas:

1. How should fund raising relate to the institution's overall priorities?

2. What is the proper relationship between the institution
   and the donor?
3. What information is the institution obligated to present
   or make available with respect to its fund raising?
4. When should a gift be refused?
5. What are the professional obligations of fund raisers to
   their institutions and to their larger communities?

Fund Raising and Institutional Priorities

*The affectation of universities is the pretense that everyone
is ethically sophisticated to start with—a striking example
of self-deception. Some companies and agencies offer formal codes of ethics, but reading a code is like reading a regulation: Unless the ideas and values are internalized, their
written form is itself a form of deception* (Payton 1988b,
p. 211).

The literature on fund raising makes much of the point that
fund raisers should not set their institution's priorities for fund
raising; they should raise money for institutional priorities.
In institutions where faculty members and administrators are
at times all too willing to articulate institutional priorities—
fund raising and otherwise—the underlying reason for such
seeming deference by the fund raiser is that each request for
support for a particular purpose is a statement about what the
institution would like to become (or remain) and that each
request is a statement about how the institution would see
itself and the world. And each accepted gift, with all of its stip-
ulations and restrictions, is a statement about what the institution is willing to become, how it is willing to see itself and
the world. Fund raisers realize, consciously or subconsciously,
that these decisions are so fundamental to the character of
the institution as to require the participation of presidents,
provosts, faculty, alumni, and governing boards.

Collectively, gifts for specific purposes can have a major
influence on an institution's shape and direction. And the
influence can easily become misaligned with the shape and
direction the institution would have taken had it received only
unrestricted gifts. This influence can perhaps be seen most
dramatically in the area of athletics; many universities have
athletics programs disproportionately grander than would oth-

erwise be the case if they were unable or unwilling to receive private support.

The influence of private support on an institution's shape can also be seen in other areas. Individual gifts are typically easier to raise for programs in engineering than for programs in the humanities. Similarly, in raising money for scholarships, an institution may find many donors willing to support business students but few who are willing to support students in social work. Should the former (who are more likely to earn large incomes after graduation) be better supported by the institution while they are students? Or, as is typically the case at least for undergraduate students, when unrestricted institutional aid is realigned so that art students have the same level of support as business students, have the intentions of the donor effectively been canceled?

In a more general sense, donors influence the values to which an institution adheres (Useem 1987). Institutions seeking the support of corporations are more likely to value their business and engineering programs (to the possible detriment of their arts and humanities programs) and to experience "organizational isomorphism" with the corporations, paying increased attention to such business functions as accounting, marketing, and public relations. Emphasizing such values convinces businesses that these colleges and universities are "good investments," but it may come at the unrecognized cost of less attention to other institutional offices, such as the library and learning resources.

Beyond balancing support for the disciplines, institutions may find that targeted gifts raise issues that blend considerations of campus concern for social justice with those of donors' intentions. Most institutions find it easier to raise funds to support men's athletics than women's athletics, yet many institutions are still struggling to fund an evolving concept of equity in athletics. If the football program receives $100,000 in private donations, what is the ethical obligation of the institution to make a comparable commitment to women's athletics, and from where should the money come? As institutions develop women's athletics programs, what are their obligations to develop mechanisms for private support for the programs? Should the investment be made on the basis of current donors' interests, on the basis of equal participation of women in athletics, or on a compensatory basis, recognizing that fund raising for women's athletics has farther to go?

Similarly, although institutions may espouse affirmative action goals for increasing the numbers of minority students, they may find it very difficult to raise the funds to provide scholarships and other forms of support to diversify the student body; they may find it more difficult to raise these funds than to raise additional funds to support areas of lower institutional priority. Put another way, increasing support for minority students may de facto not become a high institutional priority, because funds are not available to support the goal.

Because total funds available are never sufficient to support institutional priorities at an appropriate level, part of relating fund raising to the institution's overall priorities is agreeing upon an assignment of the available time and effort for fund raising that balances work for high priorities where fund raising is difficult with work for less important areas where support is easier to raise. This dilemma is illustrated in figure 1, with the institutional priority of the objective for fund raising on one axis and the effort needed to raise a dollar on the other.

Figure 1.

Institutional Priority versus Effort Needed to Raise $1.00

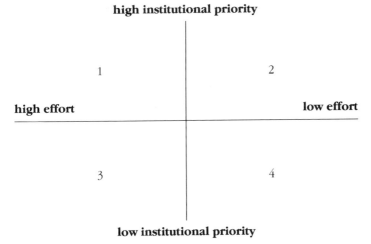

Ideally, of course, fund raisers hope to spend their efforts in the second quadrant, working on high institutional priorities where money is easy to raise. The worst case is represented by the third quadrant, where effort is directed to areas of low institutional priority and funds are relatively difficult to raise. From the standpoint of efficiency, it is difficult to rationalize devoting time and effort for fund raising to items represented by this quadrant. One can, however, rather easily imagine cases that justify spending the time and effort of fund raisers in quadrant 1 (high institutional priority but funds are difficult to raise) and quadrant 4 (low institutional priority but funds are easy to raise).

The extent to which institutions systematically consider their deployment of time and effort for fund raising along these dimensions has not been documented. Too much concern for the bottom line in fund raising discourages both fund raisers and other institutional officers from discussing the relationship between raising funds for institutional priorities versus increasing the overall amount of support raised.

The Relationship between Donor and Institution

Stanford's fund raisers likened their work to that of marketers and salespeople, matchmakers, missionaries, used car salesmen, institutional architects, and ambassadors. In all of these roles, elements of both business and drama were at play (Tobin 1984, p. 26).

Much of the language and behavior used in development suggests that the relationship between individual donors and the institution is a "gift relationship." The exchanges between donors and the institution parallel many socially accepted customs between adults in personal relationships where gifts are exchanged, as among family and close friends (Tobin 1984). The language and customs of exchanges parallel personal experience with gifts:

- The money (or property) exchanged is referred to as a *gift;*
- The sender is referred to as a *donor;*
- The recipient expresses gratitude (promptly, and as personally as possible);

- The size and frequency of gifts are at the discretion of the donor;
- Return tokens are exchanged to acknowledge the reciprocal nature of the relationship and restore balance between the two parties;
- Donors are valued for what they can give (smaller or larger amounts of money and, in the case of volunteers, time);
- In higher education, the motivation for the gift is often talked about as an expression of gratitude for what the institution, as the alma mater, has already given the donor;
- Regular donors are referred to as "friends" of the institution or members of the institution's "family"; and
- Institutions and donors seek to regularize and intensify satisfying giving relationships: Donors may give more or more frequently or give time as well as money when they feel satisfaction from the relationship; institutions give tokens, privileges of seating or presidential attention, or briefings about institutional planning or scientific progress to donors out of gratitude and to court a deeper relationship.

Yet in many ways, institutions behave toward donors in ways that would be considered inappropriate or unacceptable in personal relationships involving giving gifts:

- Institutions have developed paid staff positions in research on prospects to estimate the magnitude of the gift they might reasonably expect to receive from current or potential donors;
- "Giving clubs" are established with announced reciprocal tokens or privileges at each level of giving;
- Donors and prospective donors are asked for specific amounts of money, often for a specific purpose;
- Donors and prospective donors are "cultivated" through a series of carefully planned contacts;
- Donors are asked to give more than they have given in the past;
- Institutions regularly publish lists of donors, often organized by level of giving;
- Institutions may announce "naming opportunities" and associated costs or the size of a donation required for

naming a building or a room or establishing a named professorship or fellowship; and

- The tax benefits of giving are openly discussed with potential donors.

In some cases, the private funds do represent a gift, and the institution is the recipient. In other cases, because of the donor's motivations or the complexity of the situation, the institution acts less as the recipient of a gift and more as a partner in a contract, a seller in a purchase, a broker in an investment, or an agent that allows individuals to come to terms with life's circumstances. While support from foundations and corporations often overtly acknowledges the contractual or purchase aspects of the funds, support from individuals may also take on overtones of contracts and purchases.

Contract

Negotiations over the size and conditions of large gifts from individual donors are often so detailed that the conversation and correspondence would be unseemly as part of a personal exchange of gifts and come to resemble more closely negotiation for a contract. Indeed, restricted gifts at least have direct elements of a contract not normally present in gifts: Individuals donate money with the understanding that it will be used in specified ways. Thus, the relationship between donor and institution may be seen as a gift relationship for public and ceremonial purposes, but it also has elements of a contractual or business-type relationship, particularly in private negotiations before the actual donation.

From the institution's point of view, the degree of implied contract between the donor and the institution may vary, depending on the circumstances of the gift or its solicitation. In a general sense, appeals may imply that gifts will be used for announced purposes, as when donors are asked to give to their alma mater. Appeals that seek donations "because your support can make an important difference in so many areas—the library, faculty development, and scholarships for students" may imply a contract with the donor: Donate your gift, and we will use it for these purposes. Somewhat more specifically, capital campaigns often seek to raise large sums of money with targeted amounts for designated purposes (scholarships, the library, endowed chairs, for example). Gifts specifically designated or restricted by the donor are made with explicit understandings that the money will be used for the intended purpose.

Purchase

In some cases, when a donor makes a gift with specific returns expected, for example, the "gift" takes on more of the tone of a purchase, and sometimes the institution acknowledges it. "Naming opportunities" may suggest that the institution is selling something of value, for a price, like items that might be published in a catalog.

Are the names that appear on rooms, laboratories, and buildings simply a visible record of the donor (Bok 1982), or do they somehow record purchases of personal prominence and institutional affiliation by the donor? To what extent does the consideration of who shall receive an honorary degree take on the flavor of recognizing a "purchase" made—or seeking to "purchase" a large donation? Other temptations toward purchase include consideration for admission to the institution, proximity to athletics, and selection of board members whose potential for financial support clearly outstrips their potential for providing thoughtful leadership to the institution.

The gift-giving relationship may change and have consequences for the president of the institution:

> Many people see these [gift] relationships as mutually manipulative. It is better to be cynical about them, they say. Play to the pride of the donors, massage their egos, flatter and pamper them. Alas, all too often this works! In some cases, nothing else will work. Indeed, in some cases, only the award of an honorary degree or some other important institutional praise yields a gift. In other cases, gifts become bribes: Off the record, under cover, a donor will propose a gift in exchange, say, for admitting someone to the school (Payton 1989, pp. 37–38).

Once an ethical compromise is made, a precedent has most likely been set, and such compromises harm the integrity of the institution as well as that of the president (Payton 1989).

Some public institutions that have traditionally named buildings after devoted officers of the institution are beginning to follow the model of private institutions—naming buildings after major donors. This change in practice comes at a cost: The campus no longer records its institutional history in the names of its lecture and residence halls. By naming buildings after people who have given their money but not their professional lives to the school, public institutions may find that they have diluted the sense of campus community, often weaker to begin with at public colleges and universities.

Athletic "gifts" may come close to purchases when the perquisites of giving are items with status for which the donor would pay: privileged parking spots, desirable seating at games, or access to coaches or players. As some institutions have learned, donors may also act as though they have "purchased" influence over the direction or intensity that the athletics program will take: which coach to hire, retain, or release, which players to promote, which investments to make in the improvement of the athletics program, how prominent a place athletics should have in institutional priorities.

Investment

In other cases, the language of fund raising emphasizes a long-term outcome of personal gain to the donor's well-being. The shift has been described as a major shift in private giving from charity to philanthropy to investment. An advertisement for a fund-raising consultant proclaimed that donors want to see their money, want to gain tax advantage from giving, and want to be able to justify their contributions (back cover of *Currents*, vol. 10, no. 7). Philanthropists and those concerned with the well-being of the voluntary sector have expressed concern over the decrease in the individual level of voluntary giving but have been less likely overall to comment on the rise of the pragmatic justification for giving.

Gift relationships are polite and discreet. It is not polite for the giver to ask how the gift was used; it is not necessary, nor perhaps seemly, for the recipient to be very specific about just what the gift is needed for. With investment relationships, however, the expectations change. Investors want to know—or designate—how the gift will be used. Institutions may feel freer to hunt systematically and even aggressively for likely prospective "investors" than they would to look for donors.

This change in ascribed motivations in fund raising from those with religious or spiritual overtones to motives with pragmatic or economic overtones parallels changes noted in affirmative action. The language of justification is changing from that of social responsibility toward language of pragmatic self-interest. In affirmative action, the argument for the recruit-ment and participation of minorities has been rephrased, with the principal motive the country's self-interest in a competitive world economy. In fund raising for higher education, the argu-ment presented to alumni donors becomes that the value of one's college degree is only as good as the reputation of the alma mater; alumni should donate money to invest in the good name of the college.

... the language of fund raising emphasizes a long-term outcome of personal gain to the donor's well-being.

Agent

In receiving private funds, institutions can become the vehicle through which individuals and communities attempt to deal with the circumstances of life, a means through which indi-viduals can try to make sense of life's tragedy or good fortune. Scholarships established by donations from family and friends following a death of tragic circumstances are often explained as "trying to make some good come out of something so ter-rible." Donations from the very wealthy have been explained as motivated by the prestige associated with giving, guilt from having accumulated large amounts of wealth, the desire to immortalize one's name, or, perhaps more charitably, a good feeling from strengthening an institution or providing an opportunity to deserving students or faculty. In some cases, these donations may be thought of as gifts; in others, they may more appropriately be considered windfalls for the insti-tution that happen to be available to serve as the agent for the donor's motivations.

Similarly, in receiving support from foundations, colleges and universities are serving as agents for the fulfillment of the foundations' agendas. Foundations' wealth is accumulated from individuals, communities, and corporations, with more or less specific aims for its use. Receiving colleges and uni-versities serve as partners in supporting the arts, increasing minority access, studying health care delivery, and a host of other eleemosynary aims.

Research on prospects

Another issue about the relationship between donor and insti-tution concerns the limits of acceptable research methods on prospects. In conducting research to determine an indi-vidual's capacity to make a large gift, institutions act as inves-tors searching for potential donors in whom it is worth the institution's effort to invest time, privilege, and attention.

When fund-raising goals are high and research on prospects vigorous, a researcher may spend up to two weeks developing a profile of a prospective donor (Bailey 1988), including information on land holdings, estate and divorce proceedings, stock proxies, memberships in clubs and on corporate boards, newspaper clippings, and information from friends, business associates, and acquaintances. Prospects may also be identified or "rated" through sessions at which key members of the college community are asked to discuss the capacity to give of a pool of potential donors.

While vigorous research on prospects can be efficient and effective as a means leading to large gifts, it can lead to pragmatic difficulties: donors who become angry when they learn how much the institution knows about their finances and ethical difficulties from invasion of privacy. While the American Prospect Research Association stresses the importance of protecting the confidentiality of information, instances have been reported of fund raisers' leaving an institution with information on prospective donors and of offers from a fund raiser to sell information about the institution's donors (Bailey 1988).

Blatant difficulties aside, most institutions face a series of more frequent, routine questions about research on prospects. How vigorously can an institution investigate an individual's capacity to give without violating a relationship of trust? Is it legitimate to pursue all public sources of information? What are the limits of inquiry to friends, associates, and acquaintances? What should be done when the institution learns information that could be damaging to the individual? Is a prospect file analogous to a personnel file or transcript? That is, does the donor or the prospective donor have an ethical if not a legal right to see anything in his or her prospect file? If so, is the institution obliged ethically, if not legally, to inform the individual of this right? Despite some general injunctions not to record damaging or hearsay information in a prospect file, little in the recorded literature suggests that fund raisers have carefully considered these questions.

Sharing Information with Donors
What types of information should an institution provide or make available to donors or prospective donors? How detailed should the information be? How candid should an institution be about how its donations are used? Institutions face these

issues when there is reason to believe that the donor might not fully understand the purposes for which the solicited gift is used. Colleges in financial difficulty, for example, might use current gifts to pay past debts rather than to make new commitments, as the appeal suggests. Similarly, institutions might solicit donations to the annual fund with suggestions that the money will help support purposes like the library, scholarships, and research equipment when in fact a large proportion of the money raised will be used to support the development or alumni office and to offset the direct and indirect costs of fund raising.

Unlike separately incorporated charities that raise funds, colleges and universities are not legally obligated to report to the giving public the proportion of their unrestricted gifts that is used for the announced purposes or the proportion that might be considered overhead. While institutions, particularly public institutions, might make information available from which these proportions can be inferred, the institutions' ethical obligations in this area have been rarely systematically considered. At least one public institution found that to support the additional fund-raising costs of a capital campaign, it must tax the donations made to the campaign because no additional support was available from general revenues or tuition (Ling et al. 1988). The realization came late enough in the campaign that the institution faced questions about its obligation to tell donors whose gifts it had already accepted.

Similarly, the effect of some restricted gifts may be more diluted than donors understand. A modest gift to support scholarships for art students will typically raise the total support for scholarships by the amount of the gift while guaranteeing additional support for art students very little. Is the institution obligated to explain this relationship to the donor? Do donors want only to know that *their* money is supporting scholarships for art students? (Bok 1982). Or do some donors at least believe that they increased the total level of support for art students by the direct amount of their gift? Are institutions obliged to tell donors that while their money will support art students, their gift raised the total support available to art students by an amount far smaller than the size of the gift might indicate?

Institutions may face issues of disclosure when they seek to spend money, even from unrestricted gifts, for purposes that typical donors or less sophisticated donors might not support. Following the resignation of its president over disclosures of spending $1.7 million for home and office renovations, one large university suspended its appeals to new donors, fearing a backlash (McMillen 1988). Implicitly, some institutions have decided that it is ethically (or at least pragmatically) prudent to support activities like perquisites for presidents and athletics staff, lavish fund raisers, settlements in personnel cases, and other similar expenses only with money from donors who believe in the desirability as well as the propriety of such expenses.

Finally, institutions might feel subtle or overt pressure in the name of donor relations to mute their discussion of difficult issues. Issues of racial and ethnic intolerance and sexual harassment face many campuses. Yet, fearing a withdrawal of alumni support (as well as decreased applications from prospective students) during periods of campus unrest, colleges and universities might be reluctant to address such problems openly, to confront instances of intolerance publicly, and to act creatively to help students live and work together peacefully.

Refusing a Gift

Institutions may decide to refuse gifts for at least four reasons: (1) The source of funds may influence or appear to influence the institution's objectivity or freedom; (2) the source of money may be so "tainted" that the gift is unacceptable; (3) the restrictions on the gift (in direct or indirect costs) may be unacceptable to the institution; or (4) the institution may become unacceptably dependent on a single donor.

The principal cases in which institutions should refuse gifts, related to the first reason, are those where donors "seek to attach conditions to their gifts that invade Justice Frankfurter's 'four essential freedoms of the university'—to determine for itself on academic grounds who may teach, what may be taught, how it shall be taught, and who may be admitted to study" (Bok 1982, p. 266). These freedoms speak to the institution's academic offerings, yet they may rather easily be extrapolated to provide guidance in those cases more likely to be problematic to institutions where gifts are concerned: sponsorship of research and athletics. Table 7 suggests how Frankfurter's four essential freedoms can be translated from academics to athletics and research.

TABLE 7

WHEN DO DONATIONS ENTAIL PROBLEMS?
AN EXTENSION OF FRANKFURTER'S FOUR ESSENTIAL FREEDOMS

Academics	Athletics	Research
Who may teach	Who shall be the coach	Who will be hired to conduct research
What may be taught and at what level	What sports shall be offered	What research questions shall be addressed
How shall it be taught	How shall the coach call the plays	What methods shall be used to conduct the research
Who shall be admitted to study	Who may join the team to participate	How and where shall the results be reported

Source: Bok 1982.

In the case of funding for research where the donor might have a strong interest in the outcome of the study, alternate sources of funding might be sought or at least a suspect gift refused, yet the ultimate decision should be left to the faculty member, who has a far greater stake in upholding the reputation of his or her scholarly work than do campus administrators (Bok 1982). Institutions would typically be less likely to extend formally such independent judgment to coaches and athletics staff about which gifts to accept. The lack of formal policies, the presence of enthusiastic boosters, and several related factors, however, increase the likelihood that some inappropriate athletic gifts are accepted. And, although the National Collegiate Athletic Association has developed rules for acceptable types of support from boosters, the temptations appear largely out of sight of the development staff or the chief institutional officers.

Second, institutions might consider refusing a gift because it represents "tainted money": The donor has earned the money through immoral means or has known behavior otherwise unacceptable to the community. Refusing gifts on such grounds requires caution, however; one university president said he "never assumed accepting a gift was an affirmation of the donor's good character" (Bok 1982, p. 270). A retired president whose language was more colorful and "eager to build a great university" noted, "The Devil has had that money

long enough; I have a laundromat just outside my door"
(Bornstein 1989b, p. 6). The dilemma is as much a practical
as a philosophical problem. If an institution is to refuse a gift
based on the character of the donor, how extensive is the
responsibility to investigate and judge good character? Who
is to make the judgments and on what criteria? What is an
institution to do if it discovers at a later date that a gift
accepted in good faith was made by a donor whose character
is later determined to be unacceptable? To paraphrase George
Bernard Shaw in *Major Barbara,* institutions must either share
the world's guilt or go to another planet (Bok 1982).

While the question of accepting gift money may appear
more problematic when questions of naming are involved,
the Rhodes and Fulbright scholarships and fellowships are
valued without the recipients' (or others') feeling as though
they are endorsing the views of the donors (Bok 1982). Yet
limits are involved: "No university could accept a Hitler Col-
lection of Judaica . . . or a Capone Institute of Criminology"
(Bok 1982, p. 274). How an institution is to know when this
limit has been reached or who is to decide is left less clear.
Nor is the question of evolving standards of acceptable social
behavior given any direct attention: It is conceivable, for
example, that an institution might have named a chair (or a
building or a scholarship) several years ago for a donor whose
behavior, though acceptable at the time, is currently viewed
as unacceptable toward women or minorities or along some
other dimension.

Recently, some charitable institutions have refused planned
gifts because the financial planners contacting them about
the transaction have offered large gifts on the condition of
large fees (Stehle 1989). Fund raisers have reported discom-
fort with what they see as the financial planners' selling contributions to the highest bidder and with receiving planned
gifts motivated only by financial, not philanthropic, impulses.

Third, an institution might refuse a gift because the restrictions make the gift unacceptably expensive in direct or indirect costs. A donation of horses to start an otherwise unsup-
ported program in equine studies is one example; a donation
to fund an annual conference on art in the Middle Ages at a
technical institute is another. Rising costs for energy and maintenance have caused colleges to think carefully before accepting a gift for the direct but not indirect costs of a new building

(Kemeny 1978). A restricted gift is more difficult to refuse
if the promise or hope exists that it may be followed by a substantial unrestricted gift or one directed toward a higher institutional priority.

In general, restrictions are viewed as acceptable to the
extent that they match the institution's existing priorities and
values or at least do not conflict with them. Scholarships that
support students from Johnson County are acceptable; scholarships that support minority students are valued. But what
of the scholarship restricted to white students? Because in
fact at most institutions, such a gift would have the practical
effect of raising the total amount of scholarship aid available
to all students, the problem is not the outcome of accepting
the gift: It is the perception and the institutional conscience
that problems exist. "By accepting such a gift, the university
will associate itself in some fashion with a prejudice deeply
contrary to its ideals. . . . The administration [must] decide
if it can balance a distaste for linking itself with prejudice
against the opportunity to offer greater support for its needy
students" (Bok 1982, p. 278).

Fourth, institutions would be well advised to refuse gifts
when they risk becoming overly dependent on a single donor
or type of donor. Institutions risk high outside influence when
(1) they rely heavily on outside resources; (2) outside contributions are small in number and narrow in purpose; (3)
one or a small number of contributors account for a dispro-
portionate share of the gifts; and (4) the supply of other,
potential contributors is restricted (Useem 1987). A vivid
example of the effects of strong reliance on a single donor
is the case of the University of Rochester. With substantial
funding from and reliance on Kodak for institutional gifts and
students for its business programs, the institution withdrew
its offer of acceptance of a student who was an employee of
the rival Fuji film manufacturer, fearing breaches of corporate
security. When the issues of academic freedom and institutional independence were determined to be of greater importance, the student was readmitted, though the decision was
moot as the student had decided in the interim to attend MIT
(*Chronicle* 1987a, 1987b).

Gifts might also be refused when the institution does not
want to rely inappropriately on donors to define its shape or
priorities. When, in difficult financial times, Dartmouth cut
a major sport, the president refused gifts that would restore

it, claiming to do so would do "permanent damage" by allowing donors to determine the nature of the institution (Kemeny 1978).

Questions of when to refuse a gift are difficult in part because the institution is likely to have faculty members, students, or programs that would benefit from its decision to accept any particular gift. Refusing a gift might come with the associated costs of losing other gifts from the same donor (for more acceptable purposes), losing gifts from associates of the donor, or losing the general support and friendship of the disgruntled donor and his or her associates. Seldom does openly refusing an inappropriate gift have compensating public benefits of institutional distinction.

Obligations of Fund Raisers to the Campus and Community

What are the obligations of fund raisers to follow their own values or work to influence those of the institution? How strong is the obligation to present the institution or program candidly to the potential donor? What is the responsibility of fund raisers with special skills to work toward the larger public good beyond the institution? Can fund raisers live for philanthropy while living off it? (Payton 1988b).

In seeking support for institutional programs or the overall welfare of the institution, fund raisers are often in positions of making strong statements about what is valuable, important, or legitimate without having access to the professorial cloak of academic freedom under which to debate questions of approach or substance. One development office experienced a conflict over soliciting alumni couples who have multiple affiliations with the institution (Tobin 1984). The institution had evolved a preference system of solicitation that gives some schools preference over others and gives preference for the husband's affiliation over that of the wife.

Some fund raisers find it bothersome, or at least awkward, to defend a system that favors male graduates. On the other hand, those who uphold the system argue that policy reflects the already existing affiliation preference of Stanford alumni. They say couples contribute more readily to the husband's alma mater than to the wife's. As fund raisers, they consider it their business to be responsive to the existing social system. They have neither the power nor the respon-

sibility to change alumni's social preferences . . . (Tobin 1984, p. 37).

This example highlights several of the questions before fund raisers: To what extent should fund raisers defend practices that they find "bothersome"? To what extent should the institution develop or continue a policy that might maximize total giving while classifying their alumni preferences according to (possibly outdated) actuarial information rather than expressed personal preference? To what extent should fund raisers develop or continue a practice that will systematically generate less private support for programs that are predominantly women's areas?

Fund raisers face at least three types of situations that can bring their personal values into conflict with their perceived duties as fund raisers:

1. Questions of equity with respect to donors (as the preceding example of husband's and wife's affiliations illustrates) or with respect to the outcome of a campaign (as with men's and women's athletics);
2. Balancing institutional pressures toward improving the bottom line in fund raising with issues of matching fund raising with institutional priorities or directing fund raising toward areas of greatest need; and
3. Advising an institution (often in the person of the president) about when to refuse a large gift or when a gift comes with expectations—perhaps not explicitly stated—that could well become troublesome in the future.

The questions that face fund raisers are more difficult, because they typically face the questions alone, with little support from the institution or the profession. Institutional questions about fund raising are seldom discussed either within institutional policy-making groups or in professional development programs for fund raisers. The dilemmas of fund raising are not the central dilemmas of colleges and universities—the dilemmas that revolve around teaching and research, around truth and the freedom to pursue it.

Nor do strong external supports exist for confronting these issues. Professional fund raisers are left to confront their questions of ethics and values largely on their own without the supports available to members of the strong professions (e.g., specialized graduate training, strong professional associations that address issues beyond the pragmatic) and the tradition of institutional introspection (e.g., academic freedom). Although the Council for Advancement and Support of Education (CASE), the American Association of Fund-Raising Counsel, and the National Society for Fund-Raising Executives have developed formal codes of fair practice or ethics, the statements are so brief, each less than a page, and so general as to provide little guidance. Like many such statements, they "lack a means for the development of a definitive body of case interpretation to help specify the scope and limits of a given rule. . . . [They are] guidelines without lines to guide [and] leave unilluminated many of the quandaries and temptations practitioners face" (May 1980, p. 213).

Another dilemma fund raisers face concerns their opportunities and obligations to share their talent with the larger communities. Successful fund raisers have developed skills that can be of considerable use to other nonprofit agencies in their communities, agencies that serve the arts, health, and welfare. When fund raisers do voluntary work for another nonprofit organization, are they fulfilling a professional obligation to distribute their services justly and on the basis of need, or are they setting up a potential conflict of interest with their employer? Is their volunteer work a pro bono obligation of their field, or is it a problem of dividing their loyalty—and their effectiveness—between the institutions for which they work and the philanthropic needs of their communities? (This dilemma is similar to the one faced by many board members. Because approximately 20 percent of the members of governing boards serve on more than one board, these members are subject to potential conflicts, for they might be expected or asked to help raise funds for more than one institution from the same source [Ingram and Associates 1980].)

Fund raisers are confronted with opportunities (and temptations) to help raise funds for groups whose constituency of potential donors might compete with those of their college or whose eleemosynary goals compete or conflict with those of their college. And because fund raisers ipso facto endorse the general goals of philanthropy, they will presumably be generally more predisposed than the average person to support voluntary groups and causes.

Some development personnel work in institutions with "national" student and alumni bodies; virtually any nonprofit group for which they might contribute time and specialized knowledge could compete with some sources from which their institution might hope to raise support. Other development personnel work in institutions that draw their student body principally from the state or the local community; analogously, these professionals are typically more likely to have the opportunity to help raise support for local charitable or nonprofit groups. Arguably, at least, a fund raiser from a college with a very local student body (and alumni group) who works for a community cause is more likely to be in potential competition for funds with his or her institution than a fund raiser from a college with a national audience who works for national charities or causes.

The potential conflict fund raisers face is not often duplicated within the institution: While faculty members' consulting activities might put them in a conflict of interest with their institution's goals for public service or might engage their scholarly skills on projects for which they do not have publication rights, fund raisers have the unusual potential situation of their outside work's being in conflict with institutional work when the outside activity is *voluntary*. The institutional goals of community service or community relations suggest that fund raisers will find at least selective encouragement to share their skills beyond the campus. On the other hand, the pragmatic goals of fund raising may mitigate against the practice, at least in specific instances.

A final question of obligation to the community is raised: Do fund raisers live *for* philanthropy or do they live *off* philanthropy? (Payton 1988b). Are they "called" to their work, or are they simply employed to perform a specific task? The issue to a large extent applies to all who work in higher education: Are nonprofit organizations somehow different from other kinds of organizations because of the causes they serve? If different, are they better? If one feels "called" to work in a nonprofit organization, does that mean one is somehow "chosen" (and therefore somehow better than others who work at a more mundane level)? Is one who lives for philanthropy expected to receive less in monetary rewards because although they somehow live *for* the cause, they also live *off* it?

This distinction between living for and off a philanthropic cause raises particular tensions between paid staff and volunteers (Payton 1988b):

. . . CASE's 1985 Greenbrier II conference . . . marked the beginning of increased attention within the field to ethical issues.

- Volunteers clearly live *for,* not *off,* a cause.
- Volunteers work directly, with their own resources (time, skill, and money), whereas professional staff work indirectly, with resources supported by others.

In the extreme, fund raisers can be guilty of "the sin of pride": "arrogance . . . the self-righteousness and sanctimoniousness that is common if not rampant throughout the [voluntary] sector, on both sides of the table. It tends to inflate the moral worth of those engaged in philanthropy and to deflate the moral worth of those engaged in other forms of work, especially if that work is explicitly self-interested" (Payton 1988b, p. 88).

Yet for the professional, the work of raising support for institutional goals, of cultivating donors, of finding friends and funds for the college is full-time work, whereas for the volunteer it is typically part time. The professional may be better educated in the field and have specialized knowledge and experience in fund raising and higher education. The professional may be guided by values not widely shared within the volunteer community and may be tempted to do what he or she "knows is right" even though volunteers do not (yet) agree (Payton 1988b). Thus, the salaried professional must balance a greater knowledge of the institution's needs and full-time commitment to fund raising with the volunteer's primary interest in raising funds for a cause that brings with it no substantial direct, personal gain.

The last few years, beginning with CASE's 1985 Greenbrier II conference, have marked the beginning of increased attention within the field to ethical issues. More recently, initiatives have begun in other associations as well, including the National Society for Fund-Raising Executives, the National Committee on Planned Giving, and the American Prospect Research Association (Bornstein 1989a). At this stage, the work can be characterized by identifying issues and producing general statements of expectations; the formal models are few and the language is not completely developed.

Perhaps the broadest consideration of ethical issues to date came in a 1986 symposium organized by CASE. At those sessions, James Donahue, an ethics professor from Georgetown University, provided general guidance, including the proposal of a matrix that fund raisers might use when considering ethical issues within their own institution. The matrix has risk/

safety along one axis and harm/benefit along the other (Council for Advancement 1986). Fund raisers should aim for decisions that are in the quadrant of safety+benefit and avoid decisions in the realm of risk+harm; the other two quadrants represent the gray areas. Donahue has also suggested that the implications of a potential decision be considered in terms of the institution's mission, the potential benefits, the precedent-setting aspects, considerations of legality and truthfulness, and implications for the decision maker and others.

Beyond this session, little evidence suggests that considerations of ethical questions in fund raising have drawn upon the general theoretical thinking in ethics; the issues have not been framed within the context of general or applied normative ethics (e.g., Beauchamp and Childress 1984; Callahan and Bok 1980). For example, fund raisers do not generally consider their issues in terms of teleological theories, such as utilitarianism, which stress consideration of the known or probable outcome of one's actions, or deontological theories, which stress moral rules that may be binding regardless of the outcome. Nor have fund raisers' issues been explored within the framework of more general issues of professional ethics, which considers matters such as deception, informed consent, privacy and confidentiality, individual and collective responsibility, social responsibility and professional dissent, and social responsibility and justice (Callahan and Bok 1980). The types of dilemmas fund raisers face are within the same general categories as those other professionals face, and they may be discussed in terms of more general ethical theories. CASE has found it helpful to involve philosophers and other experts in professional ethics in their considerations of ethical issues; institutions may likewise find campus experts who can help direct locally useful discussions.

ANALYSIS, IMPLICATIONS, AND RECOMMENDATIONS

Most of our colleges appear to do better at stretching out the
needy hand than at putting forward the best foot
(Pollard 1958, p. 12).

Analysis and Implications of the Literature Review
History and trends
The most notable historical changes in fund raising in higher
education with implications for the fund-raising practitioner
include:

1. Church-affiliated solicitation and solicitation of individuals,
   which characterized educational fund raising from the
   17th century, have been replaced in the 20th century with
   increased professional efforts.
2. The notion of *charity,* central to the message and appeal
   of early fund raising, has been replaced with *philanthropy,*
   and the development of theories of donors' behavior has
   changed to acknowledge that shift.
3. While once considered optional, a fringe activity, or an
   adjunct to the duties of the president or a few trustees,
   fund raising has become a central activity in colleges and
   universities and is no longer an option, even for the new-
   est member of the American higher education family, the
   community college.
4. Once considered the preserve of independent colleges,
   programs for private voluntary support in *public* higher
   education have become accepted by both donors and
   colleges.

It seems clear that these trends are here to stay, with
increasingly more formal and centrally planned fund-raising
programs in higher education, more fund-raising programs
using principles of marketing and embracing an exchange
model of donors' behavior rather than a purely altruistic
model, and wide acceptance of the idea that competition for
private funds will come from every type of institution.

The effectiveness of fund raising
Studies that attempt to explain institutional effectiveness by
way of the institution's characteristics, including its students
and alumni, seem to have dominated research in fund raising
for the last 20 years. Close behind are studies that attempt to
explain donors' behavior using their personal characteristics.

While they represent a rather narrow focus for research, they also appear to be the most fundamental issues to professional fund raisers and to those who make institutional policies regarding fund raising and factors under administrative control that might affect the results of fund raising. However narrow they may seem, these foci seem to be where research energy ought to have been focused over the past two decades and where attention could quite fruitfully remain for the time being.

Few unqualified generalizations on effectiveness can be made from a review of the research literature other than the clear and consistent association of institutional spending with the results of fund raising. But increased spending is not the same as *wisely* increased spending, and little research can be counted on for guidance. Even if one interprets the feasibility study as an ethnographic research project, little guidance is available. Because the results of these studies are confidential and do not find their way into the research literature, institutions must conduct feasibility studies and hire fund-raising counsel as one would hire a rainmaker—largely on the basis of reputation and recommendations rather than guided by research results.

Numerous studies suggest that institutional pride, prestige, and emotional attachment by alumni are associated with more successful fund raising. They are gratifying to the fund-raising profession because, properly organized, they are part of an institution's advancement program and within access of the administrator of advancement/development. The various other factors frequently associated with successful fund raising are not under the control of the administration of the advancement program or readily altered in the interests of fund raising. The fund-raising professional is therefore wise to concentrate on amount spent on fund raising and on the advancement programs designed to enhance prestige, pride, and the emotional commitment of alumni.

Institutional spending on advancement
Studies attempting to codify or standardize spending or relate it to output are limited to surveys of spending without regard to optimal level or control of the marginal costs of fund raising. The best advice available suggests that internal rather than cross-institutional comparisons are to be preferred, with careful attention to the management of marginal costs within pro-

grams and over time, including careful monitoring of average costs, changes in marginal costs per gift dollar, diminishing returns, the percent of the total institutional budget spent on advancement, and gift income by source and program.

Donors' behavior

The models of individuals' behavior as donors showing significant promise are those that depart from purely altruistic motives in favor of exchange models, which allow for motives in the donor based on receipt of "goods" in exchange for the gift and a repeated disequilibrium that always leaves the donor with an additional need to respond to recognition with more gifts. Planning programs with this sort of model in mind as an element in shaping a marketing program would be most effective.

In general, the people more disposed to giving are married persons with children, persons declaring a religious affiliation, particularly Protestants, women, and those with more schooling, even holding income constant. Among alumni donors, increased disposition is found among the wealthier, middle-aged or older individuals (44 percent of all cash gifts to higher education from individuals come from those over 70, 88 percent from those over 50), those with strong emotional ties to their alma maters, those who have earned at least a bachelor's degree, those who participate in alumni activities, and those with religious or other voluntary affiliations. Attempts to explain donors' behavior by use of preenrollment characteristics or student activities or characteristics while a student have not been particularly fruitful except for occasional studies that find giving associated with living on campus, engagement in special activities, or receipt of (perceived) adequate financial aid. Sex and marital status have not been good predictors of donors' behavior among alumni.

Corporations' behavior as donors is clearly entwined with self-interest expressed as gains in research in the area of the company's needs, production of trained personnel, the prestige associated with giving, the resultant good public relations associated with giving, employees' morale and satisfaction, and the improvement of the community environment where the company functions.

For foundations, past successes, evidence of ability to perform, and size and prestige of the institution appear to influence decisions to contribute funds. Most foundations, being basically highly focused, thinly staffed, and conservative, are more inclined to give to well-established, older, and larger organizations and tend to follow the lead of other donors or larger foundations—possibly on the assumption that other organizations donating funds have done the necessary research to give confidence that the recipient is worthy of the gift, thus avoiding the need for further research and evaluation.

Donors of all types seem to believe in a link between price and quality and are eager to give to institutions of prestige and magnitude. With regard to tax incentives and the economy, it appears that companies and organizations respond conservatively in times of economic setback, while individuals seem to give during, if not despite, hard economic times. The wealthy, as might be expected, are most sensitive to the price of giving and respond most to changes in deductibility, while the middle class and the poorest—particularly when it comes to giving to churches—seem relatively immune to the effects of tax incentives or fluctuations in the economy.

With regard to athletics, the body of research is completely at odds with the conviction of both fund raisers and donors. No evidence of any substance suggests that success in intercollegiate athletics is associated with increased total giving to an institution or to athletic giving other than in the most limited time periods or in anecdotal cases. This conviction, that successful athletic teams breed successful fund raising, will no doubt withstand the myriad research evidence to the contrary, as athletic boosters want so desperately to believe it and most advancement officers and presidents use athletic events to cultivate donors.

With regard to organization, it appears that almost all coordinated and centralized development activity in higher education is less than 40 years old, with only 25 percent of all institutions reporting a centralized development function as recently as 1970. Organizational character varies enormously from institution to institution and from type to type, except that certain common characteristics were found in 75 percent or more of colleges in one comprehensive survey, confirming that the best advice of the gurus of the organization of fund raising for higher education is being followed.

Ethical considerations faced by fund raisers help define institutions' mission and shape and the relationships institutions have with some of their most important constituencies.

Decisions that institutions make about what private support to pursue or accept help define their mission and boundaries. Private support solicited or received can influence colleges and universities in ways more significant than is typically recognized. By extending gift relationships to relationships that more resemble contracts, purchases, or investments, fund raisers help redefine the relationship between institutions and their friendly supporters. At a time when technology and aggressive techniques extend the boundaries of what institutions can learn about their prospective benefactors, institutional supporters may raise their own expectations about how much strategic information they expect from institutions where they are investing their own resources. What donors expect to know about institutions to which they are giving a gift of gratitude may differ substantially from their expectations from an institution in which they see themselves making an investment or with which they are establishing a contractual relationship. Finally, fund raisers face questions of their relationship with their own institution and the extent to which their professional commitment to voluntary fund raising can or should extend to a personal commitment.

Areas of Suggested Research and Improved Techniques and Strategies

An Agenda for Research on Fund Raising provides a concise and exciting focus for research on fund raising (Carbone 1986a). The first order of business it calls for is a review of extant research, to which this review is a partial response. Now, four years after the conference that was the basis for that monograph, Carbone's list still looks like the best prescription for strengthening the body of knowledge, making the literature more professional, and addressing the information needed by fund raisers and decision makers in higher education. Briefly summarized, the agenda includes research on:

- *The philanthropic environment,* including studies of philanthropic organizations, motivational and behavioral studies of donors and nondonors, analytical studies about the nature of philanthropy, sociological studies of philanthropy, and case studies of the impact of fund raising on institutions of higher education.

- *The work and careers of fund raisers,* including studies of role perception and role definition of individuals involved in fund raising, motivational studies of volunteers, studies of compensation of fund raisers, task analysis and psychological studies of those involved in raising funds, and the effectiveness, job satisfaction, and career paths of fund raisers.
- *The management of fund raising,* including organizational studies of fund raising, an analysis of the content of materials produced to support fund raising, studies of the influence of fund-raising programs on other institutional programs, cost-benefit studies, studies of the involvement of consultants in institutional fund raising, policy studies of national, state, and institutional regulations that affect fund raising, application of market research techniques to fund raising, studies of planning for and evaluation of fund raising, studies of the structures and environments of institutional fund raising, and case studies of specific fund-raising programs or techniques conducted by cohorts of similar institutions (Carbone 1986, pp. 27–36).

Additional approaches, strategies, and areas of inquiry can be identified from this review for the most probable high return on energy invested. The following suggestions can add crucial information to the development of an integrated theory of fund raising, donors' behavior, and effectiveness of fund-raising practices.

Consistency of variables and measures used
It is imperative that common terms, definitions, and operational constructs be employed. Studies of institutional effectiveness can seldom be compared because of the wide differences in institutions and the considerably liberal assumptions about proxy variables of institutional quality— to take only one example—that have been made. In some studies, the quality variable is proxied by the median SAT score of entering students, in others, national academic quality ratings are applied, and in still others, institutional expenditures per student are employed. Differences in the interpretation of the role of quality in such studies are difficult if not impossible to explain and only cloud other characteristics (public versus private, research versus liberal arts, and so on)

that might better explain or be related to differences in effectiveness.

A major tool for research on cost-effectiveness is *Management Reporting Standards for Educational Institutions* (Council for Advancement 1982). Developed in conjunction with the National Association of College and University Business Officers, the guidelines for reporting expenditures and revenues provide the basis for consistent definition for researchers, but the literature does not yet include substantial numbers of studies using the consistent definitions of the standards.

Consistency and follow-up in research

Follow-up studies should refine and improve a previous research project, strengthen the inferences to be drawn by narrowing or broadening the sample, and correct those details or data elements overlooked in the original design of the research. A rather surprising finding from this review is the very small number of research studies that the same or other researchers followed up on. This review found very few *second* research publications by an author, little or no follow-up research projects, and, more disconcerting, far too many *un*published dissertations. The reason is perhaps that most of the disciplined research on fund raising is done by graduate students completing a doctorate. Often these students have conducted their work without the benefit of a major professor whose own scholarly inquiry is focused in the area of fund raising for higher education. Once completed, the dissertation may be published, but the professional fund raiser has no time—or no incentives at work—to continue with follow-up studies that could refine findings or correct inadequacies in the original research. The quick pace of fund raising, with its emphasis on concretely measurable success, and the lack of rewards or professional peer interest in one's scholarship militate against integrating continued scholarship in the life of the practicing fund raiser.

A further problem with consistency and follow-up is that until very recently, no colleges or universities were identified with a scholarly program in fund raising or with a reasonably steady stream of dissertation research conducted under a few major professors following a clear course toward the development of theory. Most dissertations appear to emanate in higher education administration programs, and the choice

fund raising . . . is increasingly linked to the larger context of philanthropic and voluntary activity.

of the topic of *fund raising* is more likely based on the student's employment in the field of development rather than on an organized research program sparked and stewarded by the interests of the graduate faculty.

Prospects and Resources for Future Research

Over the next decade, several factors are likely to improve both the quantity and the quality of research that can inform fund raising in higher education. First, as fund raising becomes more important within a larger number of institutions, its identification as a topic of research will probably increase. Within universities, scholars from anthropology to marketing to philosophy to psychology have developed theories that can be tested and refined in the laboratory of educational fund raising, and as fund raising becomes more visible on campuses and more important to collegiate constituencies, a likely spin-off is increased scholarly attention from local researchers.

Second, a number of research universities have established centers or other identifiable scholarly activity on philanthropy, voluntarism, and nonprofit organizations, several of which show a direct interest in matters related to fund raising for higher education: Yale University's Program on Nonprofit Organizations, Duke University's Center for the Study of Philanthropy and Voluntarism, and Indiana University–Purdue University at Indianapolis's Center on Philanthropy. Additional efforts have been identified at Case Western Reserve University, City College of New York, and the University of Maryland. Some of the work at these institutions has been supported by foundations, most notably the Exxon Education Foundation and the Lilly Endowment.

Third, as the professional organizations that serve fund raisers grow stronger and more mature, they are developing the capacity to help the membership think beyond the techniques of fund raising and link them with relevant scholarly work. For example, CASE has broadened its staff, conference programs, awards programs, and publications to include research, and the American Association of Fund-Raising Counsel recently published a substantial insert in its newsletter on the history and meaning of philanthropy to acquaint readers with "philanthropy in a comprehensive sense" (Gurin and Van Til 1989, p. 3). And, as noted earlier, several professional organizations have undertaken projects related to the ethical dilemmas that confront their members. Fund raisers who understand their societal context and begin to see research that can inform practice will tend to increase their expectations of scholarly work.

Fourth, fund raising in higher education is increasingly linked to the larger context of philanthropic and voluntary activity. The strongest link comes from the work of the Independent Sector, which represents over 600 voluntary organizations and affiliated interests. Two of its projects are particularly helpful to fund raisers in higher education: the Spring Research Forum, which results in the publication of the annual Working Paper (Independent Sector and United Way Institute 1988a, 1988b), and an annual compilation of research in progress of scholarly work in philanthropy, voluntary action, and other not-for-profit activity. Both publications contain work that is relevant to scholars in fund raising for higher education, and both are available through the ERIC system.

These four factors provide ample cause for optimism that fund raising in higher education will increasingly be informed by research useful to the practitioner and by scholarly thought that helps connect today's challenges and dilemmas with the larger context of America's philanthropic and voluntary traditions.

Suggestions for Research
Some suggested areas for research are offered here as they derive from the review of research.

Research on consistency of college mission
The study conducted by the Women's College Coalition suggests that a possibly fruitful area of inquiry is colleges that are perceived by their potential and actual donors as having remained consistent with regard to mission. In this country, hundreds of institutions have abandoned (or grown out of) their original missions, some with considerable debate and dispute by alumni. Some have abandoned (or been abandoned by) their church affiliations, and others have elected not to change despite growing economic and social pressures. Are the alumni of colleges whose missions have remained consistent more likely to remain loyal and demonstrate their support financially, as appears to be the case with women's colleges? Are the colleges that appear to have remained faithful more likely to enjoy the sustained faith of their graduates?

Are those that have clung to long-standing, and possibly anachronistic, missions lost support from potential new sources, while maintaining only traditional ones? Have colleges that have refocused their missions cultivated new support at the expense of traditional ones? Studies addressed to such questions will encounter the obvious problems of defining new and old support and of partitioning effects that are the result of time alone, increases or decreases in advancement effort, or the possible effect of consolidation of focus (i.e., the effect that with fewer remaining colleges devoted to a particular mission, the remaining supporters have fewer outlets for their support). But a properly devised research design should accommodate these possibilities and provide very useful insight for institutions contemplating such changes.

Research on spending and effectiveness of fund raising

Institutional spending seems associated, after the fact, with more effective fund raising. But increased spending is not synonymous with *wisely* increased spending. Energetic research needs to be applied to examining the returns on a variety of approaches to increased effort, comparing and contrasting the returns under reasonably comparable conditions and institutional types. Does doubling the number of nights of phonathons at a cost of $50,000 yield a better increase than hiring a second corporate and foundation relations officer with the same $50,000? Does increasing the frequency of the alumni magazine at a cost of $20,000 outweigh the impact of personalized solicitation letters at the same cost?

Research on roles of governance and trustees

The public sector has tended to imitate the tried and true methods developed by private colleges with decades more experience. Many elements of that experience have not been subjected to empirical test, most notably the stress placed on trustees' leadership and participation in fund raising. The character of public institutions with politically appointed boards might warrant a different role for trustees in fund raising; perhaps the role of public boards is primarily to ensure that private fund raising is supported within the institution (Farley 1986). Many public board members are appointed not as guardians for the college and advisers to the president but as advocates of the state's budget and advisers to the governor or legislative leadership. Although a public institution might be advised to appoint the trustees of its own foundation to serve in a fund-raising role (Gale 1989), no data exist as to the effectiveness of this arrangement or the extent to which these trustees can approach the success of fund raising of governing board members in private institutions. The assumption, that if trustees' leadership is important in fund raising in private institutions, then trustees' leadership—of the governing board or the foundation—is important in public institutions, has not been systematically tested.

Research on attitudes of alumni

Some research studies have linked the emotional commitment of alumni to the institution as a correlate to donative behavior, and some general studies have similarly linked all types of donors' behavior to emotional ties to the institution supported. While many studies have attempted to link undergraduate experiences (e.g., Greek life, athletics, residence, student clubs, and activities) to the behavior of donors, none have linked the formation of attitude and emotional links to post-graduation experiences. Should a college advancement office attempt to cultivate positive attitudes among the alumni through publications, reunions, and bonding events, it would be important to know just how mutable is the attitude established during undergraduate days. Are attitudes toward the college relatively set by commencement time? Can postgraduate contact with alumni do more than exploit already established attitudes, or can attitudes be changed? The answers to these questions could guide advancement offices in targeting efforts at cultivation by determining the return likely from such efforts.

Evaluation as research

Evaluations of programs conducted with research-like rigor can be immediately useful for decision making and can form the basis for broader generalizations for other institutions. For over 20 years, the American Educational Research Association has recognized institution-specific evaluation as a valuable form of research and evaluation as itself a fit subject for a special interest group within the association. The American Evaluation Association is dedicated to the improvement of the methodology of evaluation, and the Association for the Study of Higher Education and the Association for Institutional

Research recognize and support the presentation and publication of studies using evaluation techniques.

Miniresearch projects, designed to test in a single institution whether, for example, paid student callers to nondonors outperform volunteer callers, can provide immediate and practical results. Cumulatively, across several similar institutions, such evaluations can answer that question with increasingly broader generalizations, particularly if the institutions adopt general principles for conducting evaluations. Evaluations of programs should be conducted using research techniques, and these results should be shared among peer institutions and published through clearinghouses so that they might inform more practitioners and form the basis for more intense research.

Research on segmented markets

Investigators of fund raising in higher education have naturally been drawn to studies of donors' behavior, just as practitioners have longed for a simple list of characteristics that could help them identify likely donors from longer lists. As indicated earlier, the cumulative results of these studies have been somewhat disappointing, given their relatively high numbers. These studies have tended to survey all alumni of a single (or small group) of colleges or to inquire among such a narrow range of alumni (e.g., by age or undergraduate major), however, that it is difficult if not impossible to distinguish their responses from those that might be gained from a larger group.

Researchers and practitioners alike might find greater gains by thinking of potential alumni donors as belonging to "segmented markets," with distinguishable subgroups to which different messages might make the most effective appeals. The use of focus groups and the analysis of survey results by subgroups should be explored more systematically than has been done to see whether this approach will yield useful results. Although the greatest use of segmented markets currently developing among fund raisers is in fund raising among constituencies (typically organized by the professional school attended or major pursued), the popularity of programs of giving to athletics suggests that other powerful constituencies or market segments may exist.

One way to explore for possible subgroups would on the basis of the years of college attendance. Student culture and subcultures within an institution exert powerful influences on the undergraduate experience (Horowitz 1987; Moffat 1989). To some extent, each generation of students invents its own culture; what appealed to students of the 1960s may be fairly different from what appeals to students of the 1990s, and those differences are likely to remain for some years after graduation, muted by the influence of age and postcollege experiences. Institutions are encouraged to think carefully about what variables are likely to identify important "segments" of their alumni markets.

Broadened questions and methodology

As noted earlier, much of the research on fund raising in higher education has taken the form of surveys to discover characteristics of effective institutions or to uncover descriptions of alumni donors; other analyses have been done by economists to derive models that explain charitable giving.

The interesting questions on fund raising—and the methodologies to pursue them—far exceed this modest list. Questions of culture and the language of fund raising can be pursued using theories and techniques derived from anthropology, organizational theory, communication theory, and linguistic analysis. Studies of subcultures and techniques from market research can be particularly useful as institutions move toward fund raising among constituencies. Advanced graduate students working as interns or faculty members who can be enticed into working in an on-campus laboratory can bring their specialized expertise to broaden the questions addressed through research and share their insights on campus as well as with their scholarly peers.

Recommendations to Institutions

The following recommendations to colleges and universities are offered as suggestions for strengthening their programs of fund raising based on available research and inquiry.

- *Consider sources of private support strategically, deciding which sources have the best potential for a particular institution.*

In recent years, the active practice of fund raising has spread from the elite private colleges and universities to elite public universities, from a broader range of private institutions to a broad spectrum of public colleges and universities and most recently to public community colleges. Yet the advice to institutions on developing successful programs of fund raising is largely undifferentiated by such salient institutional characteristics as control, size, age, student body, degree level, location, and mission. These characteristics are as likely to be important in matters of fund raising as they are in matters of recruiting students and designing curriculum.

The tradition of fund raising is strongest in older, more selective private liberal arts colleges, in elite private universities, and in women's colleges. These institutions, along with a few lead public universities, tend to have well-established capacities for development and to be successful in raising private funds from a variety of sources. They also have access to networks of similar institutions with which they can share information and at least estimate the relative strengths and weaknesses in their portfolios of fund-raising capacity and effectiveness. Large numbers of institutions, however, including community colleges and historically black institutions, have short histories in active fund raising and limited support within the institution in terms of experienced staff and well-organized records of alumni and friends.

In assessing their capacity to raise private funds, these less experienced institutions in particular would be well advised to consider their strategic advantage in seeking support from various sources. The most effective way to increase private giving among institutions without a strong history in the area is likely to be different for a public community college in a large city, a church-affiliated liberal arts college in a small town, and a regional state college that was formerly a normal school.

For example, although many institutions consider their alumni to be the first, logical source of private donations, investing in developing a strong alumni office may not be a wise choice for public community colleges (Smith 1986). Public community colleges tend to be young institutions; many community college graduates who are the most financially successful may feel strong allegiance to the four-year institution from which they graduated, and alumni records are often poor. Many community colleges may find greater return on their investment in development from developing strong ties with local industry. In 1987–88, while corporations represented 23 percent of total private support for all institutions, among public community colleges, corporations represented 45 percent of all private support (Council for Aid 1989). Drawing upon the industries' wish for a well-prepared work force, community colleges can develop relationships that include grants of equipment and donations, sponsorship of special events, and other individual and corporate gifts that come from close affinity with the institution as a whole or special relationships with a particular program.

Similarly, for many institutions, investing fund-raising resources in programs for deferred giving may be more effective than a comparable investment seeking to raise funds from private foundations. For example, 40 percent of the community colleges with the largest endowments report that the endowments have been built mainly from bequests or trusts (Smith 1986).

For all institutions, the timing and strategy for seeking support should vary with the audience. Alumni donors are more likely to give when the perceived need of their alma mater is high; economic analyses suggest that an optimal time to approach alumni donors is when the general economic signs are poor and that at any time the message should include the importance of "individual support to maintain or enhance institutional quality or prestige" (Leslie et al. 1983, p. 224). On the other hand, corporate giving is likely to be higher when the economy is good and when taxation is perceived to be low. The suggested message for fund raisers is to emphasize the healthy economy and the role of higher education in its growth.

- *Designate some private support for areas that will build students' understanding of the importance of private support for colleges and universities.*

Although the research is not conclusive, some evidence indicates that students' own involvement with their learning and with campus life may be a predictor of their later habits of donation to their alma mater. To the extent that such relationships are real and causal, institutions should consider designating a portion of their donations for activities that directly link students to campus and making sure students are aware that these special opportunities were made available through private donations from alumni; examples might include "residence" scholarships for students who would otherwise commute, programs to support out-of-class interaction between faculty and students, and support for training student leaders. It may be helpful to structure recognition events where students meet and thank personally representative alumni and other benefactors.

- *Develop academic and other programmatic ways to enhance students' eleemosynary habits.*

Many institutions have developed giving programs for graduating seniors and student alumni associations to initiate the habit of giving in prospective alumni. While the initial results of such efforts, as indicated by senior pledges, are encouraging, no longitudinal data have been reported to indicate long-term success.

A smaller number of institutions, some with support from the Association of American Colleges, have begun to teach students about philanthropy. The courses described are approached from perspectives as varied as philanthropy as an aspect of American capitalism to philanthropy as a life of service to others (Payton 1988b), and a growing network of resources is available to faculty members interested in designing such courses (Payton 1988a). By using the campus's efforts at advancement as a laboratory and the academic perspectives of the faculty for theoretical and philosophical considerations, institutions have important opportunities to increase students' understanding of and commitment to the traditions of philanthropy.

- *Work to strengthen the tradition of philanthropy and community service.*

Higher education participates in the voluntary sector in two important ways: community service and fund raising. In the case of community service, institutions make voluntary contributions to the well-being of the larger community: Lectures and facilities are open to the public, faculty members provide free consultation to schools, community agencies, and small businesses, and students volunteer their time to help children, the needy, and the aged. In the case of raising funds, the institution receives the voluntary contributions of money and time for its well-being. Both to maintain this country's strong tradition of broad participation in the voluntary sector and to increase the type of support that comes through unrestricted gifts, colleges and universities are motivated to support the reciprocal activities of philanthropy and community service.

Colleges and universities have two fundamental motivations to support the voluntary sector, one pragmatic and one philosophical. From a practical standpoint, voluntary gifts help support the institution's vitality and, in some cases, its existence; community service helps the institution justify its tax-exempt status in cities and states and helps soothe relations between town and gown. From a philosophical point of view, institutions of higher education are motivated to support the voluntary sector as a way to strengthen the community. Many colleges and universities embrace the goal of helping students develop the values of community and community service, of working toward charity and justice, and of making a contribution beyond their family life and employment. Through their community service and their fund raising, institutions share their resources with the community-at-large and encourage others to give to the community of the institution.

Higher education participates in the voluntary sector in two important ways: community service and fund raising.

• *Participate in locally useful research studies.*

While the calls for stronger and more systematic research on educational fund raising promise long-term benefits to professionals in development and alumni affairs, locally developed studies may offer the greatest return on investment in the near future. Clues to an institution's success in and potential for fund raising can best be gathered from candidly sharing information within peer groups of institutions and by monitoring costs (including marginal costs) versus revenues over a period of time.

Agreements among peer institutions to share information on fund raising arise naturally out of groups formed for other purposes. Affiliations of region, size, control, and mission mean that these groups' information on fund raising can naturally control for some of the variables most difficult to "control" in research but most powerful in explaining patterns of private support. By agreeing on variables of interest and common definitions of those variables, peer groups can begin to share data as well as informal reports of plans and results of fund raising.

Plans for long-term institutional data can be developed jointly by the chief fund-raising officer, the institutional researcher, and the chief financial officer. Important internal considerations include the amount of private support raised by source (measured in constant dollars), the average cost to raise a dollar, and the marginal cost to raise a dollar (to calculate the real increase in support raised when efforts are increased). In addition, while it is important to estimate not only the direct cost of fund raising associated with each category of fund-raising, it may also be useful to estimate the indirect cost (such as the involvement of the president and other key administrators). Other variables of interest in institutional research include the average gift, the average gift per person solicited, the proportion of solicited alumni who give, the average gift per FTE student, and the endowment per FTE student. These variables, of interest to the institution, may also form a basis for sharing information within a peer group of institutions.

- *Develop an active way to deal with values and ethical issues in fund raising.*

Institutions can develop local statements and procedures to ensure that their fund raising is in harmony with the institution's values and priorities. Senior fund-raising staff should develop institutional statements of policies and procedures for dealing with ethical issues, sharing these written guidelines with staff and volunteers, developing a climate in which institutions can deal with difficult issues openly when they arise, and leading by example (Bornstein 1989a). Broad participation within the institution in the development and refinement of such policies and procedures may also help balance the drive within institutions for their fund-raising staff's success with the bottom line.

Recommendations to Associations and Foundations

- *Broaden professional development conferences and workshops, going beyond the techniques of fund raising.*

While the short-term success of fund raisers depends on successfully mastering and implementing the techniques of generating private support, the long-term success of the enterprise requires that fund raisers address questions of ethics and values, strategic planning, and research and evaluation. Fund raisers should be helped to address these topics within their own groups and to engage institutional and scholarly researchers in continuing lines of research that will inform the theory and develop the practice of fund raising. As fund raisers come to understand the history and significance of American traditions of philanthropy and voluntary action, they have a larger context in which to understand their work and to explain its significance within their institution and to donors and volunteers.

- *Establish opportunities for reflection on practice, such as sabbaticals and study leaves, and programs for visiting scholars and practitioners.*

Practitioners should have the opportunity for study leaves of a few weeks to several months to work on fund-raising research, to reflect and write from the wisdom of practice, and to teach courses on philanthropy to undergraduate and graduate students. The quick pace of fund raising, the emphasis on concretely measurable success, and the lack of a scholarly or reflective tradition in practice make it unlikely that such opportunities will be available without outside support from professional associations and foundations.

- *Continue and strengthen the developing support for research in fund raising and efforts to integrate philanthropy into the curriculum.*

The Lilly Endowment, the Exxon Education Foundation, the Independent Sector, and the Council for Advancement and Support of Education, among others, have recently initiated programs that encourage and support research in fund raising and the development of academic coursework on philanthropy, voluntarism, and institutional advancement. The opportunities for broad participation, for multiple perspectives on key issues, and for scholars to work cooperatively can all help strengthen these efforts.

- *Lead and support institutions in shaping their fund raising to reflect recent and projected demographic changes.*

Demographic changes in society and in higher education will require new perspectives for successful fund raisers and funding agencies. The issues are complex and lack systematic attempts to address them, as the issue of gender illustrates. Over half of the students in higher education today are women, women control large amounts of wealth, and with more women working, more women have their own earned assets as potential gifts to higher education. Yet foundations have traditionally been reluctant to fund programs that support programs specifically targeted to females; a recent report indicates that only about 3 percent of foundation gifts are so targeted (Goss 1989a). And while women's colleges have had increasing success in their own fund raising (Women's College Coalition 1988), little or no research is available to indicate whether any institutional priorities would appeal particularly to women donors. Further, with growing numbers of women in key fund-raising positions and growing evidence of their success, concern has been expressed that the feminization of fund raising may harm the status and pay of professionals in the field (Goss 1989b). The changing demographics, the problems, and the opportunities associated with issues of gender have such potentially significant effects on fund raising that the questions deserve the careful attention of professional associations and foundations.

Issues of ethnicity and race are no less complex or important. By 2000, several states will be populated by a majority of minority group members. The impact on higher education is already being felt, and the dramatic effects will increase over the next generation. Yet the tradition of financial support to colleges and universities has not been well established among most minority groups. Recent efforts by minority entertainment and athletic leaders with large, highly publicized gifts to higher education are one very visible attempt to illustrate the importance of support for higher education. But very little is known about the potential for support from various minority groups or the most effective means of strengthening their traditions of giving to higher education.

With growing interactions among nations, fund raising too is becoming internationalized. Lead institutions are seeking and receiving increased private support from their alumni and private corporations, particularly in Japan and in European countries. While the potential to increase support seems high, institutions are finding challenges of cultural differences, communication, and logistics as they translate their American techniques to other countries (Gadzik 1989).

- *Include research and evaluation as special interest groups within professional organizations, in their publications, and on the agendas of their national and regional meetings.*

CASE has taken some significant steps: the appointment of a research director, establishment of a national research council, research awards, and other increased efforts to spotlight research. Increased attention will not only stimulate those who can and will conduct research; it will also make the non-research practitioner aware that the research goes on, has some role in the profession, and informs practice.

Summary
This report has outlined the available knowledge, represented through competent research discovered in a comprehensive review. Although somewhat disappointing, valuable findings that can be interpreted to a practitioner in a form that can inform practice have been identified. In addition, an agenda for future research and organizational strategies has been prescribed to help fill the gap in available knowledge.

While fund raising in America is nearly as old as higher education itself, the last 30 years have seen both an enormous expansion of institutional fund raising and a unifying conception of fund raising as part of an institution's overall efforts at advancement. With the support of professional associations, foundations, and major university centers, fund raisers for higher education in the next decades are likely to see a marked increase in the store of scholarly knowledge available to help them plan, evaluate, and interpret their work. And as an increasing spectrum of institutions comes to depend on the "margin of excellence" or the "investment in the future" that private support can bring, fund raisers are also likely to experience a broader understanding and acceptance of their aims and techniques throughout the institution, among faculty as well as presidents, among young alumni as well as major donors.

REFERENCES

The Educational Resources Information Center (ERIC) Clearinghouse on Higher Education abstracts and indexes the current literature on higher education for inclusion in ERIC's data base and announcement in ERIC's monthly bibliographic journal, *Resources in Education* (RIE). Most of these publications are available through the ERIC Document Reproduction Service (EDRS). For publications cited in this bibliography that are available from EDRS, ordering number and price code are included. Readers who wish to order a publication should write to the ERIC Document Reproduction Service, 3900 Wheeler Avenue, Alexandria, Virginia 22304. (Phone orders with VISA or MasterCard are taken at 800/227-ERIC or 703/823-0500.) When ordering, please specify the document (ED) number. Documents are available as noted in microfiche (MF) and paper copy (PC). If you have the price code ready when you call EDRS, an exact price can be quoted. The last page of the latest issue of *Resources in Education* also has the current cost, listed by code.

Alberger, Patricia. 1980. "Tapping Student Talent: How to Get the Best from the Brightest." *CASE Currents* 6(11): 10–12.

Allem, Warren A. 1968. "Devices That Business Corporations Have Used in Supporting Higher Education." Ed.D. dissertation, Columbia Univ.

Amdur, Neil. 1971. *The Fifth Down: Democracy and the Football Revolution.* New York: Coward, McCann & Geohagen.

American Association of Fund-Raising Counsel Trust for Philanthropy. May/June–July/August 1989. *Giving USA Update.* New York: Author.

Andreoni, James R. 1986. "Essays on Private Giving to Public Goods." Ph.D. dissertation, Univ. of Michigan.

Bailey, Anne L. 30 September 1988. "Today's Fund-Raising Detectives Hunt 'Suspects' Who Have Big Money to Give." *Chronicle of Higher Education:* A1+.

———. 2 May 1989. "United Way Contributions up 6.9 Percent; Schools and Colleges Suffer a Drop." *Chronicle of Philanthropy:* 1.

Bakrow, William John. 1961. "The Relative Effectiveness of Certain Procedures and Practices in Fund Raising in Selected Private Colleges and Universities." Ed.D. dissertation, Indiana Univ.

Balz, Frank. 1987. *Donors to Higher Education: A Statistical Profile of Individual Giving.* Washington, D.C.: National Institute of Independent Colleges and Universities. ED 284 507. 20 pp. MF-01; PC-01.

Bargerstock, Charles Thomas. 1982. "An Historical-Legal Analysis of the Influence of Public Policy on Gifts from Individuals to Institutions of Higher Education." Ed.D. dissertation, Lehigh Univ.

Beauchamp, Tom L., and James P. Childress. 1984. "Morality, Ethics, and Ethical Theories." In *Ethics, Education, and Administrative Decisions,* edited by Peter A. Sola. New York: Peter Lang Publishing.

Beckett, Ray Herbert, Jr. 1973. "The Meaning, Management, and

Benefits of a Deferred Gifts Program for Public Institutions of Higher Learning in the Intermountain West." Ph.D. dissertation, Univ. of Utah.

Beeler, Karl Joseph. 1982. "A Study of Predictors of Alumni Philanthropy in Private Universities." Ph.D. dissertation, Univ. of Connecticut.

Bell, Joyce M. 1977. "A Study of the Persuasive Speaking Techniques of Private Black College and University Presidents in Their Fund-Raising Efforts for Survival." Ed.D. dissertation, North Texas State Univ.

Bennett, Richard L., and John C. Hays. 1986. "Setting Targets for a Successful Capital Campaign." In New Directions for Institutional Research No. 5, edited by John A. Dunn. San Francisco: Jossey-Bass.

Blumenfeld, Warren S., and P. L. Sartain. 1973. "Development and Cross-validation of a Psychometric Procedure to Forecast Alumni Donation Behavior: Market Segmentation in a Fund-Raising Context." Proceedings of a meeting of the American Psychological Association.

———. 1974. "Predicting Alumni Financial Donation." *Journal of Applied Psychology* 59(4): 522–23.

Bok, Derek. 1982. *Beyond the Ivory Tower: Social Responsibilities of the Modern University.* Cambridge, Mass.: Harvard Univ. Press.

Bornstein, Rita. 1989a. "The Capital Campaign: Benefits and Hazards." In *The President and Fund Raising,* edited by James L. Fisher and Gary H. Quehl. New York: Macmillan.

———. 1989b. "Ethics in Fund-Raising Planning." Paper presented at the CASE Winter Institute for Senior Development Professionals, February, Miami, Florida.

Boulding, Kenneth E. 1973. *The Economy of Love and Fear.* Belmont, Cal.: Wadsworth Publishing.

Bremner, Robert H. 1988. *American Philanthropy.* 2d ed. Chicago: Univ. of Chicago Press.

Brooker, George, and T.D. Klastorin. 1981. "To the Victors belong the Spoils." *Social Science Quarterly* 64(4): 744–50.

Buck, Joseph A., III. 1976. "Perceptions of Selected Corporate Officials in Five Southeastern States Which Influence Their Corporation's Giving to Higher Education." Ed.D. dissertation, Univ. of Georgia.

Budig, Jeanne E. 1976. "The Relationships among Intercollegiate Athletics, Enrollment, and Voluntary Support for Public Higher Education." Ph.D. dissertation, Illinois State Univ.

Callaghan, Dennis W. 1975. "Management of the Corporate Gift-Giving Function: An Empirical Study in the Life Insurance Industry." Ph.D. dissertation, Univ. of Massachusetts.

Callahan, D., and S. Bok, eds. 1980. *Ethics Teaching in Higher Education.* New York: Plenum Press.

Callahan, Lois A., and G.M. Steele. 1984. "Securing Business and Industry Support for Community Colleges: A Follow-up Study on the California Association of Community Colleges Commission on Vocational Education 1982 Statewide Voc Education Study." ACCCA Management Report 1984-5/1. ED 250 018. 78 pp. MF-01; PC-04.

Carbone, Robert F. 1985. "Class Act." *Case Currents* 11(8): 40–41.

———. 1986a. *An Agenda for Research on Fund Raising.* College Park: Univ. of Maryland, Clearinghouse for Research on Fund Raising.

———. 1986b. *A Supplement (1982–1986) to* Research in Institutional Advancement: *A Selected, Annotated Compendium of Doctoral Dissertations.* Washington, D.C.: Council for Advancement and Support of Education.

———. 1987. *Fund Raisers of Academe.* College Park: Univ. of Maryland, Clearinghouse for Research on Fund Raising.

———. 1989. *Fund Raising as a Profession.* College Park: Univ. of Maryland, Clearinghouse for Research on Fund Raising.

Carlson, Joann. 1978. "The Role of Alumni in the Financial Survival of Independent Education." Ed.D. dissertation, Univ. of California–Los Angeles.

Carnegie, Andrew. 1900. *The Gospel of Wealth and Other Timely Essays.* New York: Century Company.

Cheatham, Roy E. 1975. "A Study of Financial Support Provided by Selected Private Foundations to Historically Black Colleges and Universities." Ph.D. dissertation, St. Louis Univ.

Cheit, Earl F., and Theodore E. Lobman. 1979. *Foundations and Higher Education: Grant Making from Golden Years through Steady State.* Technical Report for the Ford Foundation and the Carnegie Council on Policy Studies in Higher Education. ED 167 169. 150 pp. MF-01; PC-06.

Chronicle of Higher Education. 9 September 1987a. "U. of Rochester Cancels Admission of Employee of a Kodak Competitor": A1+.

———. 16 September 1987b. "U. of Rochester Readmits Employee of Kodak Competitor": A1+.

———. June 1988. "Wheaton College Agrees to Return Gifts to Donors Who Object to Co-education": A1.

Clotfelter, Charles T. 1980. "Tax Incentives and Charitable Giving: Evidence from a Panel of Taxpayers." *Journal of Public Economics* 13: 319–40.

———. 1985. *Federal Tax Policy and Charitable Giving.* Chicago: Univ. of Chicago Press.

Community Health Foundation. 1976. "Fund Raising." ED 145 889. 30 pp. MF-01; PC-02.

Connolly, Michael S., and Rene Blanchette. 1986. "Understanding and Predicting Alumni Giving Behavior." In New Directions for Institutional Research No. 5, edited by John A. Dunn. San Francisco: Jossey-Bass.

Cook, Diana. 1988. "An Initial Investigation of Knowledge, Skills, and Values of Newly Employed Development Officers in Higher Education." Ph.D. dissertation, Univ. of Akron.

Council for Advancement and Support of Education. 1982. *Management Reporting Standards for Educational Institutions: Fund Raising and Related Activities.* Washington, D.C.: Author. ED 230 161. 23 pp. MF-01; PC-01.

———. 1985. *Greenbrier II: A Look to the Future.* Washington, D.C.: Author.

———. 1986. *Asking the Right Questions: Ethics and Institutional Advancement.* Washington, D.C.: Author.

Council for Aid to Education. 1989. *Voluntary Support of Education: 1987–88.* New York: Author. HE 023 058. 87 pp. MF-01; PC-04.

Council for Financial Aid to Education. 1979. "How to Develop an Effective Program of Corporate Support for Higher Education." ED 206 248. 24 pp. MF-01; PC-01.

———. 1987. *Voluntary Support of Education: 1985–86.* New York: Author. ED 288 461. 169 pp. MF-01; PC-07.

Curti, Merle E., and Roderick Nash. 1965. *Philanthropy in the Shaping of American Higher Education.* New Brunswick, N.J.: Rutgers Univ. Press.

Cutlip, Scott M. 1965. *Fund Raising in the United States: Its Role in America's Philanthropy.* New Brunswick, N.J.: Rutgers Univ. Press.

Dahl, Randall W. 1981. "Early Predictors of Alumni Giving: An Empirical Study of Selected Pre-Enrollment Characteristics and Collegiate Career Experiences in the Giving Behavior of Alumni of a Public University." Ed.D. dissertation, Univ. of Kentucky.

Dean, Joseph Oral, Jr. 1985. "Educational Fund Raising in Church-Affiliated Colleges: A Predictive and Prescriptive Model." Ph.D. dissertation, Univ. of Alabama.

Dietz, Larry H. 1985. "Iowa State University Alumni Contributions: An Analysis of Alumni Giving Patterns by Selected Class Years—1974 and 1979." Ph.D. dissertation, Iowa State Univ.

Douglas, James. 1983. *Why Charity? The Case for a Third Sector.* Beverly Hills, Cal.: Sage.

Drachman, Sally. 1983. "Factors Accounting for Variations in Levels of Private Giving to Higher Education in the United States." Ph.D. dissertation, Univ. of Arizona.

Dunn, John A., Jr., ed. 1986. "Enhancing the Management of Fund Raising." In New Directions for Institutional Research No. 51. San Francisco: Jossey-Bass.

Duronio, Margaret A., B. Loessin, and G. Borton. 1988a. "A Common Notion about Fund-Raising Success: Myth or Fact?" Working Paper No. 4. Paper presented at an AIR Forum, May, Phoenix, Arizona. ED 298 858. 26 pp. MF-01; PC-02.

————. 1988b. "A Survey of Fund-Raising Methods: Implications for Management." Working Paper No. 5. Paper presented at a meeting of the American Educational Research Association, April, New Orleans, Louisiana. ED 296 651. 29 pp. MF-01; PC-02.

Duronio, Margaret A., B. Loessin, and R. Nirschel. 1989. "The Price of Participation." *CASE Currents* 4(15): 39–44.

Dye, Richard F. 1986. "Fund Raising in Small Colleges: Strategies for Success." *Sources for Higher Education: Taxes and Other Determinants* (special issue, Economics of Education Finance) 5(2): 191–95.

El-Khawas, Elaine. 1985. "Campuses Weld the Corporate Link." *Educational Record* 66(2): 37–39.

England, Thomas G. 1973. "Influence of Student Protest upon Philanthropic Support of Selected Institutions of Higher Education." Ed.D. dissertation, Univ. of Tennessee.

Evans, Gary A. 1989. "Financing the Development Program." In *The President and Fund Raising*, edited by James L. Fisher and Gary H. Quehl. New York: Macmillan.

Evans, Jeanette H. 1986. "A Study of the Attitudes of the Alumni of Historically Black Colleges and Universities toward Financial Giving to Their Alma Maters." Ed.D. dissertation, Morgan State Univ.

Farley, Eileen. 1986. "Fund Raising and Public College Trustees." *AGB Reports* 28(5): 22–23.

Feldstein, Martin. 1975. "The Income Tax and Charitable Contributions. Part I. Aggregate and Distributional Effects." *National Tax Journal* 28: 81–99.

Fey, John T., S. Fuller, and R. Payton. 1977. "The Corporate Stake in Higher Education: An Underdeveloped Potential." ED 207 419. 23 pp. MF-01; MC-01.

Fisher, James L. 1986. "The Growth of Heartlessness: The Need for Studies on Philanthropy." *Educational Record* 67(1): 25–28.

————. 1989. "Establishing a Successful Fund-Raising Program." In *The President and Fund Raising*, edited by James L. Fisher and Gary H. Quehl. New York: Macmillan.

Frederick, Robert E. 1984. "Intercollegiate Football Success and Institutional Private Support: A National Study of 81 Public Universities, 1965–1979." Doctoral dissertation, Univ. of Kansas.

Frey, James H. 1985. "The Winning-team Myth." *CASE Currents* 11(1): 33–35.

Gabrielsen, Paul T. 1975. "Increasing Financial Support of Small Private Colleges through Model Fund-Raising Programs." Ph.D. dissertation, U.S. International Univ.

Gadzik, Tanya. 22 November 1989. "Fund Raisers at U.S. Colleges Broaden Their Horizons, Seek Gifts from Companies and Alumni Overseas." *Chronicle of Higher Education:* A21+.

Gale, Robert L. 1989. "The Role of the Governing Board." In *The President and Fund Raising*, edited by James L. Fisher and Gary

H. Quehl. New York: Macmillan.

Gallagher, M. Eymard. 1964. "A Study of Private Two-Year College Fund-Raising Programs." Ed.D. dissertation, Teachers College, Columbia Univ.

Gardner, Paul M. 1975. "A Study of the Attitudes of Harding College Alumni with an Emphasis on Donor and Nondonor Characteristics." Ph.D. dissertation, Ohio Univ.

Gaski, John F., and M. Etzel. 1984. "Collegiate Athletic Success and Alumni Generosity: Dispelling the Myth." *Social Behavior and Personality* 12(1): 29–38.

Gillespie, Bonnie J. 1983. "Financing Traditionally Black Institutions of Higher Education." ED 234 113. 33 pp. MF-01; PC-02.

Glennon, Mary A. 1985. "Fund Raising in Small Colleges: Strategies for Success." Ed.D. dissertation, George Washington Univ.

———. 1986. "Fund Raising in Small Colleges: Strategies for Success." *Planning for Higher Education* 14(3): 16–29.

Goss, Kristin A. 4 April 1989a. "Foundations Accused of Spending Too Little on Problems of Women." *Chronicle of Philanthropy* 1(12): 1+.

———. 21 March 1989b. "Influx of Women into Fund Raising Poses Paradox: They're Effective, but Pay and Prestige Could Suffer." *Chronicle of Philanthropy* 1(11): 1+.

Goulden, J.C. 1971. *The Money Givers.* New York: Random House.

Grace, Judith D. 1988. "Good Sports? Three Studies Examine Athletic Fund-Raising Programs." *CASE Currents* 14(7): 59–60.

Gurin, Maurice G., and Jon Van Til. May/June–July/August 1989. "Understanding Philanthropy: Fund Raising in Perspective." *Giving USA Update:* 3–10.

Haddad, Freddie Duke, Jr. 1986. "An Analysis of the Characteristics of Alumni Donors and Nondonors at Butler University." Ed.D. dissertation, Butler Univ.

Hall, Peter Dobkin. February 1989a. "Beyond the Filer Commission." *Philanthropy Monthly:* 23–26.

———. January 1989b. "Dilemmas of Nonprofit Research." *Philanthropy Monthly:* 11–13.

Harris, James T. 1988. "An Assessment of Factors Related to Successful Fund Raising at Public Doctorate-Granting Universities." Ph.D. dissertation, Pennsylvania State Univ.

Heeman, Warren, ed. 1979. *Analyzing the Cost-Effectiveness of Fund Raising.* New Directions for Institutional Advancement No. 3. San Francisco: Jossey-Bass.

Hodgkinson, Virginia A., and Murry S. Weitzman. 1986. *The Charitable Behavior of Americans: A National Survey.* Washington, D.C.: Independent Sector.

Hollingsworth, Patricia. 1983. "An Investigation of Characteristics of Successful Community College Foundations." ED 233 756. 25 pp. MF-01; PC-01.

Hopkins, E.H. 1958. "The Advancement of Understanding and Support of Higher Education." The Greenbrier Conference Report on Organizational Principles and Patterns of College and University Relations. Washington, D.C.: American College Public Relations Association.

Hornbaker, Lawrence D. 1986. "Effectiveness of Institutional Advancement Programs in Representative California Public and Private Colleges and Universities." Ed.D. dissertation, Pepperdine Univ.

———. November 1987. Interview in "What Are the Characteristics of a Successful College Development Program?" *Taft Nonprofit Executive.*

Horowitz, Helen L. 1987. *Campus Life: Undergraduate Cultures from the End of the Eighteenth Century to the Present.* New York: Alfred A. Knopf.

Hunter, T. Willard. 1975. *What Motivates Large Gifts?* Washington, D.C.: Brookings Institution.

Independent Sector. 1988. *Research in Progress, 1986–87: A National Compilation of Research Projects on Philanthropy, Voluntary Action, and Not-for-Profit Activity.* Washington, D.C.: Author. ED 301 124. 572 pp. MF-02; PC-23.

Independent Sector and United Way Institute. 1987. *The Constitution and the Independent Sector.* Proceedings of the Spring Research Forum. Washington, D.C.: Author. ED 302 111. 511 pp. MF-02; PC-21.

———. 1988a. *Looking Forward to the Year 2000: Public Policy and Philanthropy.* 1988 Spring Research Forum Working Papers. Washington, D.C.: Author. ED 301 126. 696 pp. MF-04; PC-28.

———. 1988b. *Philanthropy and the Religious Tradition.* 1989 Spring Research Forum Working Papers. Washington, D.C.: Author.

Ingram, Richard T., and Associates. 1980. *Handbook of College and University Trusteeship.* San Francisco: Jossey-Bass.

Isherwood, Alex C. 1986. "A Descriptive Profile of the Fund-Raising Programs in NCAA Division I-A." Doctoral dissertation, Univ. of Maryland.

Ishoy, Victor A. 1972. "Fund Raising: A Function of Development in Financing Higher Education." Ed.D. dissertation, Brigham Young Univ.

Jacobson, Harvey K., B. Mack, and J. Dean. 1986. "Setting the Agenda in Fund-Raising Research: Lessons from Contrasting Strategies." Paper presented at an AIR forum, June, Orlando, Florida. ED 280 388. 28 pp. MF-01; PC-02.

Jefferson, Nickey L. 1985. "Institutional Advancement at Land-Grant Universities." Ph.D. dissertation, Univ. of Missouri at Columbia.

Jencks, Christopher. 1987. "Who Gives to What?" In *The Nonprofit Sector: A Research Handbook,* edited by Walter W. Powell. New Haven, Conn.: Yale Univ. Press.

Jordan, Milton Edward. 1985. "Guidelines for the Evaluation of Fund

Raising at Private Postsecondary Institutions." Ph.D. dissertation, Univ. of Florida.

Keller, Mary J.C. 1982. "An Analysis of Alumni Donor and Nondonor Characteristics at the University of Montevallo." Ph.D. dissertation, Univ. of Alabama.

Kelly, Kathleen S. 1979. "Predicting Alumni Giving: An Analysis of Alumni Donors and Nondonors of the College of Journalism at the University of Maryland." M.A. thesis, Univ. of Maryland.

Kemeny, John G. January 1978. "Why a President Might Refuse a Million Dollar Gift." *CASE Currents* 4: 27.

Korvas, Ronald James. 1984. "The Relationship of Selected Alumni Characteristics and Attitudes to Alumni Financial Support at a Private College." Ph.D. dissertation, Univ. of Missouri–Kansas City.

Lawrence, William. 1926. *Memories of a Happy Life*. Boston: Houghton Mifflin.

Lawson, William B. 1976. "Foundations and Private Institutions of Higher Education: A Merging of Interests or a Parting of the Ways?" Ph.D. dissertation, Arizona State Univ.

Lederman, Douglas. 13 January 1988. "Do Winning Teams Spur Contributions? Scholars and Fund Raisers Are Skeptical." *Chronicle of Higher Education* 34(18): A1+.

Lemish, Donald L. 1981. *The Foundation Handbook: A Private Foundation Approach to Fund Raising at State Colleges and Universities.* ED 214 484. 34 pp. MF-01; PC not available EDRS.

Leslie, John W. 1979. "Variations in Fund-Raising Potential among Colleges and Universities." In *Analyzing the Cost-Effectiveness of Fund Raising,* edited by W. Heeman. New Directions for Institutional Advancement No. 3. San Francisco: Jossey-Bass.

Leslie, Larry L. 1985. "What Appeals to Whom? Donors Respond to Different Approaches." *CASE Currents* 11(7): 34–37.

Leslie, Larry L., S. Drachman, G. Ramey, and C. Conrad. 1983. "Factors Accounting for Variations over Time in Voluntary Support for Colleges and Universities." *Journal of Education Finance* 9(2): 213–25.

Leslie, Larry L., and G. Ramey. 1985. "When Donors Give: How Giving Changes in Good and Bad Times." *CASE Currents* 11(9): 25–26.

———. 1988. "Donor Behavior and Voluntary Support for Higher Education Institutions." *Journal of Higher Education* 59(2): 115–32.

Lindenmann, Walter K. February 1983. "Who Makes Donations?" *CASE Currents:* 18–19.

Ling, Deidre A., V. Minor, C. Murray, and A. Rich. 1988. "Deans, Development, and Dollars: Setting the Agenda for Institutional Fund Raising." Paper presented at an annual meeting of the National Association of State Universities and Land-Grant Colleges, November, Dallas, Texas.

Loessin, Bruce A., Margaret A. Duronio, and Georgina L. Borton. 1986.

"Measuring and Expanding Sources of Private Funding." In New
Directions for Institutional Research No. 51, edited by John A.
Dunn. San Francisco: Jossey-Bass.

———. 1987. "Identifying Peer Institutions for Comparative Evaluation of Fund-Raising Effectiveness." Working Paper No. 2. Paper
presented at the 1987 AIR Forum, Kansas City, Missouri.

———. 1988a. "Fund-Raising Effectiveness in Higher Education."
Working Paper No. 3. Pittsburgh: Univ. of Pittsburgh.

———. 1988b. "Understanding Fund-Raising Effectiveness in Higher
Education: Laying a Foundation." Working Paper No. 1. Final report
prepared for the Exxon Education Foundation. Pittsburgh: Univ.
of Pittsburgh.

Luskin, Bernard J., and I. Warren. 1985. "Strategies for Generating
New Financial Resources." New Directions for Community Colleges 13(2): 73–85.

McGinnis, Dennis R. 1980. "A Study of Fund-Raising Programs at
Selected State Colleges and Regional Universities." Ed.D. dissertation, Univ. of Georgia.

MacIsaac, Charles R. 1973. "Attitudes of Donors at Selected Institutions of Higher Education." Ph.D. dissertation, Iowa State Univ.

Mack, Bruce A. 1983. "Foundation Fund Raising by Private Liberal
Arts Colleges." Ph.D. dissertation, Univ. of Michigan.

McKee, Dale F. 1975. "An Analysis of Factors Which Affect Alumni
Participation and Support." Ed.D. dissertation, Indiana Univ.

McKeown, Mary P., and Alexander Kern. 1986. *Values in Conflict:
Funding Priorities for Higher Education.* Seventh Annual Yearbook
of the American Education Finance Association. Cambridge, Mass.:
Ballinger.

McKinney, Ricardo J. 1978. "Factors among Select Donors and Nondonors Related to Major Gifts to a Private University." Ed.D. dissertation, Univ. of Miami.

McKinney, Ricardo J., R. Williams, and T. Goodwin. 1979. "Factors
among Select Donors and Nondonors Related to Major Gifts to
a Private University." ED 172 607. 16 pp. MF-01; PC-01.

McMillen, Liz. 13 April 1988. "U. of Minnesota Slows Fund-Raising
Effort Following President's Resignation." *Chronicle of Higher Education:* A36.

McNally, Frederick E. 1985. "An Analysis of Alumni Philanthropy
Related to Personal, Academic, and Social Characteristics." Ed.D.
dissertation, Univ. of San Francisco.

Markoff, Richard M. 1978. "An Analysis of the Relationship of Alumni
Giving and Level of Participation in Voluntary Organizations: A
Case Study." Ph.D. dissertation, Univ. of Toledo.

Marts, Arnaud C. 7 July 1934. "College Football and College Endowment." *School and Society* 40: 14–15.

May, William F. 1980. "Professional Ethics: Setting, Terrain, and
Teacher." In *Ethics Teaching in Higher Education,* edited by D.

Callahan and S. Bok. New York: Plenum Press.

Mays, Sylvia, and D. Vogler. 1985. "The Linkage between Community Services and College Development." *Community Services Catalyst* 15(3): 10–13.

Melchiori, Gerlinda S. *In press* a. "Alumni Research: An Introduction." New Directions for Institutional Research, edited by Gerlinda S. Melchiori. San Francisco: Jossey-Bass.

———. *In press* b. "Applying Alumni Research to Fund Raising." New Directions for Institutional Research, edited by Gerlinda S. Melchiori. San Francisco: Jossey-Bass.

Meyer, James D. 1971. "A Study of Fund-Raising Programs at Selected Institutions of Higher Education in the United States." Ed.D. dissertation, Univ. of Wyoming.

Milki, Mimi A. 1978. "An Analysis of Student Foundation Programs in Institutions of Higher Education in the U.S." Ph.D. dissertation, North Texas State Univ.

Mitchell, Maurice. January/February 1982. "Big-Time Sports Should Be Banished from the Campus." *The Center Magazine* 15: 22–24.

Moffat, Michael. 1989. *Coming of Age in New Jersey: College and American Culture.* New Brunswick, N.J.: Rutgers Univ. Press.

Moore, H. Martin. 1987. "A Model of Cooperation." *Case Currents* 13(7): 34–37.

Nielsen, Waldemar A. 1985. *The Golden Donors.* New York: E.P. Dutton.

Nusz, Phyllis J. 1986. "Development of Guidelines for the Establishment and Operation of a California Community College Foundation." Ed.D. practicum, Nova Univ. ED 273 315. 75 pp. MF-01; PC-03.

Owen, David. August 1982. "State of the Art in Panhandling." *Harper's:* 35.

Paton, George J. 1983. "Correlates of Successful College Fund Raising." Ph.D. dissertation, Stanford Univ.

———. November 1985. "Research about Development: Reasons for It, Obstacles to It." *Fund Raising Management:* 42–49.

———. 1986. "Microeconomic Perspectives Applied to Development Planning and Management." In *Enhancing the Management of Planning,* edited by John A. Dunn. New Directions for Institutional Research No. 51. San Francisco: Jossey-Bass.

Payton, Robert L. 1988a. "On Discovering Philanthropy." *Change* 20(6): 33–37.

———. 1988b. *Philanthropy: Voluntary Action for the Public Good.* New York: American Council on Education/Macmillan.

———. 1989. "The Ethics and Values of Fund Raising." In *The President and Fund Raising,* edited by James L. Fisher and Gary H. Quehl. New York: Macmillan.

Pickett, William L. 1977. "An Assessment of the Effectiveness of Fund-

Raising Policies of Private Undergraduate Colleges." Ph.D. dissertation, Univ. of Denver.

Pokrass, Richard J. 1988. "Corporate Giving to Two-year Colleges." *CASE Currents* 14(1): 38–40.

Pollard, John. 1958. *Fund Raising in Higher Education.* New York: Harper & Bros.

Pray, Francis C., ed. 1981. *Handbook for Educational Fund Raising: A Guide to Successful Principles and Practices for Colleges, Universities, and Schools.* San Francisco: Jossey-Bass.

Providence Journal-Bulletin. 12 December 1988. "Villanova Paying a Price for Accepting Donations."

Ramsden, Richard J. 1979. "The COFHE Development Study." In *Analyzing the Cost-Effectiveness of Fund Raising,* edited by Warren Heeman. New Directions for Institutional Advancement No. 3. San Francisco: Jossey-Bass.

Reingen, Peter H. 1982. "Test of a List Procedure for Inducing Compliance with a Request to Donate Money." *Journal of Applied Psychology* 67(1): 110–18.

Richards, Michael D., and G. Sherratt. 1981. *Institutional Advancement Strategies in Hard Times.* AAHE-ERIC Higher Education Report No. 2. Washington, D.C.: American Association for Higher Education. ED 207 475. 55 pp. MF-01; PC-03.

Rowland, A. Westley. 1978. *Research in Institutional Advancement: A Selected Annotated Compendium of 200 Doctoral Dissertations in Institutional Advancement.* Washington, D.C.: Council for Advancement and Support of Education.

Rudolph, Frederick. 1962. *The American College and University.* New York: Vintage Books.

Sader, Carol H. 1986. "The Role of Elected Trustees of Public Institutions in Successful Development Programs." ED 266 841. 7 pp. MF-01; PC-01.

Schwartz, Robert. 1970. "Personal Philanthropic Contributions." *Journal of Political Economy* 78: 1264–90.

Sherratt, Gerald R. 1975. "A Study of the Methods and Techniques Used in Fund Raising at Selected Public Universities." Ph.D. dissertation, Michigan State Univ.

Sigelman, Lee, and S. Bookheimer. 1983. "Is It Whether You Win or Lose? Monetary Contributions to Big-Time College Athletic Programs." *Social Science Quarterly* 64: 347–59.

Sigelman, Lee, and R. Carter. 1979. "Win One for the Giver? Alumni Giving and Big-Time College Sports." *Social Science Quarterly* 60(2): 284–93.

Smith, J.P. 1981. "Rethinking the Traditional Capital Campaign." In *Handbook for Educational Fund Raising: A Guide to Successful Principles and Practices for Colleges, Universities, and Schools,* edited by Francis C. Pray. San Francisco: Jossey-Bass.

Smith, Nanette J. 1986. "Organizational Models of Successful Advancement Programs." Paper prepared for the CASE Advancing Two-year Institutions Conference, Alexandria, Virginia. ED 278 435. 32 pp. MF-01; PC-02.

Spaeth, Joe L., and A.M. Greeley. 1970. *Recent Alumni and Higher Education.* New York: McGraw-Hill.

Springer, Felix. 1974. "The Experience of Senior Colleges That Have Discontinued Football." In *An Inquiry into the Need for and Feasibility of a National Study of Intercollegiate Athletics,* edited by George H. Hanford. Appendix I. Washington, D.C.: American Council on Education.

Stehle, Vince. 1989. "Charities Balk at Financial Planners' Demands for Finder's Fees Linked to Clients' Gifts." *Chronicle of Philanthropy* 1(12): 1+.

Steinberg, Margery S. 1984. "Marketing in the Corporate Board Room: A Study of Corporate Fund Raising for Higher Education." Ph.D. dissertation, Univ. of Connecticut.

Stout, Glen W. 1977. "A Study of Fund-Raising Programs at Selected Public Multicampus Universities." Ed.D. dissertation, Univ. of Tennessee–Knoxville.

Sweeney, Robert D. 1982. *Raising Money through Gift Clubs: A Survey of Techniques at 42 Institutions.* Washington, D.C.: Council for Advancement and Support of Education. ED 215 642. 76 pp. MF-01; PC not available EDRS.

Sweeney, Sandra S. 1982. "An Analysis of Selected Exchange Relations and Transactions between a College of Nursing and a Selected Public—Its Alumnae." Ph.D. dissertation, Univ. of Iowa.

Taussig, Michael K. 1967. "Economic Aspects of the Personal Income Tax Treatment of Charitable Contributions." *National Tax Journal* 20: 1–19.

Teitelbaum, Robert D. 1979. "How to Find Out What It's Really Costing You to Operate All Those Fund-Raising Programs." In *Analyzing the Cost-Effectiveness of Fund Raising,* edited by Warren Heeman. New Directions for Institutional Advancement No. 3. San Francisco: Jossey-Bass.

Tobin, Katherine C. 1984. "The Language of Request: Annual Gift Giving to a University." Ph.D. dissertation, Stanford Univ.

Turk, Judy VanSlyke. June 1986. "The Changing Face of CASE." *CASE Currents* 11: 8–23.

Useem, Michael. 1987. "Corporate Philanthropy." In *The Nonprofit Sector: A Research Handbook,* edited by Walter W. Powell. New Haven, Conn.: Yale Univ. Press.

Van Til, Jon. 1988. *Mapping the Third Sector: Voluntarism in a Changing Social Economy.* New York: Foundation Center.

Webb, Charles H. 1982. "A Policy-Relevant Study of Development Programs at Representative Institutions within the State University of New York." Ph.D. dissertation, Michigan State Univ.

Weber, Nathan, ed. 1988. *Giving USA: The Annual Report on Phi-*

lanthropy for the Year 1987. New York: American Association of Fund-Raising Council Trust for Philanthropy.

Welch, Patrice A., ed. 1980. *Increasing Annual Giving.* New Directions for Institutional Advancement No. 7. San Francisco: Jossey-Bass.

White, Arthur H. 1986. "The Charitable Behavior of Americans." In a Yankelovich, Skelly, and White survey commissioned by the Rockefeller Brothers Fund. Washington, D.C.: Independent Sector.

Whitehead, Paul J. 1976. "Some Economic Aspects of Corporate Giving." Ph.D. dissertation, Virginia Polytechnic Institute and State Univ.

Williams, Roger L., and R. Hendrickson. 1986. "In Fund Raising, Prestige Means More Than Public or Private." *AGB Reports* 28(6).

Williams, Ruthann E. 1981. "Career Patterns of Women in Educational Fund-Raising Administration in Colleges and Universities in the United States." Ph.D. dissertation, State Univ. of New York at Buffalo.

Willmer, Wesley K. 1980. "An Assessment of the Institutional Advancement Processes at Selected Small, Independent Colleges in the United States." Ph.D. dissertation, State Univ. of New York at Buffalo.

————. 1981a. "The Institutional Advancement Process at the Small College." In *Advancing the Small College,* edited by W.K. Willmer. New Directions for Institutional Advancement No. 13. San Francisco: Jossey-Bass.

————. 1981b. *The Small College Advancement Program: Managing for Results.* Washington, D.C.: Council for Advancement and Support of Education. ED 205 148. 155 pp. MF-01; PC not available EDRS.

————, ed. 1981c. *Advancing the Small College.* New Directions for Institutional Advancement No. 13. San Francisco: Jossey-Bass.

————. 1985. "A Large View of Small Colleges." *Case Currents* 11(7): 18–21.

————. 1987a. *Friends, Funds, and Freshmen for Christian Colleges.* Washington D.C.: Christian College Coalition.

————. 1987b. *New Look at Managing the Small College Advancement Program.* Washington D.C.: Council for Advancement and Support of Education. ED 279 234. 127 pp. MF-01; PC not available EDRS.

Wilmoth, Dirk. 1987. "The Effect of the Giving Club Threshold on Alumni Annual Giving." Ph.D. dissertation, Univ. of Rochester.

Winship, Addison L., II. 1984. *The Quest for Major Gifts: A Survey of 68 Institutions.* Washington, D.C.: Council for Advancement and Support of Education. ED 248 802. 61 pp. MF-01; PC not available EDRS.

Wisdom, Paul E. 1989. "Another Look at Costs." In *The President and Fund Raising,* edited by James L. Fisher and Gary H. Quehl. New York: Macmillan.

Women's College Coalition. 1988. *Alumnae Giving at Women's Colleges: A Ten-year Report.* Washington, D.C.: Author.

Woods, Janet. 1987. "Factors Associated with Gift Income in Public Research and Doctoral-Granting Institutions." Doctoral dissertation, Washington State Univ.

Worth, Michael J., ed. 1985. *Public College and University Development: Fund Raising at State Universities, State Colleges, and Community Colleges.* Washington, D.C.: Council for Advancement and Support of Education. ED 256 197. 170 pp. MF-01; PC not available EDRS.

Ylvisaker, Paul N. 1987. "Foundations and Nonprofit Organizations." In *The Nonprofit Sector: A Research Handbook,* edited by Walter W. Powell. New Haven, Conn.: Yale Univ. Press.

INDEX

A

Academic freedom, 71
Affirmative action, 59
Agent, 65
Alumni
        characteristics as students, 39, 40
        emotional attachment, 80
        institutional pride, 80
        prestige, 80
        social preferences, 73
Alumni funds, 8
Alumni giving, 8
        prediction, 39, 40
Alumni solicitation, 8
Alumni wealth, 22
American Alumni Council, 27
American Association of Fund-Raising Counsel, 13, 74, 86
American College Public Relations Association, 27
American Educational Research Association, 89
American Evaluation Association, 89
American philanthropy, 5
American Philosophical Society, 6
American Prospect Research Association, 66
American Red Cross, 12
Association of American Colleges, 94
Athletics, 57, 82
Average endowment, 17

B

Bequests, 15
Black colleges, 8, 23, 39, 53
Book of the Dead, 5
Brown, Nicholas, 7
Bucknell, 46

C

Capital campaigns, 17, 18
Carnegie Corporation, 11
Case Western Reserve University, 86
Catholic giving, 36
"Cause-related advertising", 10
"Cause-related marketing", 10
Charity, 6
Charity theory, 34
Chief development officer, 24
Church-affiliated solicitation, 79
Church-related schools, 23

values, 55
Fund-raising brochures, 6
Fund-raising offices, 15
Fund-raising organizations, 12, 13

G
General Electric, 47, 48
    "Corporate Alumnus Program", 48
Georgetown University, 76
Gift sizes, 62
    negotiations, 62
Gifts of annuity, 8
Giving and age, 40
"Gospel of Wealth", 11
"Greenbrier Report", 27

H
Harvard College, 6, 17
Harvard Endowment Fund Campaign, 12
Harvard, John, 7
Higher education, 5
    advancement, 27
    corporate support, 48
    development, 27
    foundation support, 11
Honorary degrees, 63

I
"Impure altruism", 34
Independent colleges, 18
Indiana University-Purdue University, 86
Individual giving, 9
Influence of donors, 58
Insurance policies, 15
Institutional fund raising, 19
    data, 28
    effectiveness, 19, 28
    effectiveness adjusted for potential, 19-21, 29
    objectively defined effectiveness, 19, 20
    perceived effectiveness, 19, 20
    studies, 19-21
    variables, 19, 21-22
Institutional independence, 71
Institutional priorities, 56
Institutional spending, 29
Investment, 64

Supreme Court of New Jersey, 9
Surveys of spending, 80

T

"Tainted money", 63, 69
Tax advantages
  and donor behavior, 40
  corporate, 13
The Economy of Love, 33
TIAA, 11
Total spending, 31
  normative data, 31
Tufts, Charles, 7
Trusts, 15
Two-year colleges, 15, 52, 53

U

Union Carbide, 48
United Fund Drive, 12
University of Chicago, 7, 17
University of Maryland, 86
University of Rochester, 71
University of Vermont, 8
Unwanted gifts, 56

V

Villanova University, 56
Voluntary giving, 5
Voluntary service, 5
Voluntary support
  colleges and universities, 14, 22
  tables, 16
Voluntary traditions, 5

W

Ward and Hill Associates, 12
Westinghouse, 47
Wheaton College, 55
Williams College
  Society of Alumni, 8
Women, 36
Women's College Coalition, 38, 87
World War I, 12

Y

Yale, Elihu, 7
Yale University, 6

YMCA, 12

ASHE-ERIC HIGHER EDUCATION REPORTS

Since 1983, the Association for the Study of Higher Education (ASHE) and the Educational Resources Information Center (ERIC) Clearinghouse on Higher Education, a sponsored project of the School of Education and Human Development at The George Washington University, have cosponsored the *ASHE-ERIC Higher Education Report* series. The 1990 series is the nineteenth overall and the second to be published by the School of Education and Human Development at the George Washington University.

Each monograph is the definitive analysis of a tough higher education problem, based on thorough research of pertinent literature and insitutional experiences. Topics are identified by a national survey. Noted practitioners and scholars are then commissioned to write the reports, with experts providing critical reviews of each manuscript before publication.

Eight monographs (10 before 1985) in the ASHE-ERIC Higher Education Report series are published each year and are available on individual and subscription basis. Subscription to eight issues is $80.00 annually; $60 to members of AAHE, AIR, or AERA; and $50 to ASHE members. All foreign subscribers must include an additional $10 per series year for postage.

To order single copies of existing reports, use the order form on the last page of this book. Regular prices, and special rates available to members of AAHE, AIR, AERA and ASHE, are as follows:

Series	Regular	Members
1990	$17.00	$12.75
1988-89	15.00	11.25
1985-87	10.00	7.50
1983-84	7.50	6.00
before 1983	6.50	5.00

Price includes book rate postage within the U.S. For foreign orders, please add $1.00 per book. Fast United Parcel Service available within the U.S. at $2.50 for each order under $50.00, and calculated at 5% of invoice total for orders $50.00 or above.

All orders under $45.00 must be prepaid. Make check payable to ASHE-ERIC. For Visa or MasterCard, include card number, expiration date and signature. A bulk discount of 10% is available on orders of 15 or more books (not applicable on subscriptions).

Address order to
ASHE-ERIC Higher Education Reports
The George Washington University
1 Dupont Circle, Suite 630
Washington, DC 20036
Or phone (202) 295-2697
Write for a complete catalog of ASHE-ERIC Higher Education Reports.

1989 ASHE-ERIC Higher Education Reports

1. Making Sense of Administrative Leadership: The 'L' Word in Higher Education
   Estela M. Bensimon, Anna Neumann, and Robert Birnbaum

2. Affirmative Rhetoric, Negative Action: African-American and Hispanic Faculty at Predominantly White Universities
   Valora Washington and William Harvey

3. Postsecondary Developmental Programs: A Traditional Agenda with New Imperatives
   Louise M. Tomlinson

4. The Old College Try: Balancing Athletics and Academics in Higher Education
   John R. Thelin and Lawrence L. Wiseman

5. The Challenge of Diversity: Involvement or Alienation in the Academy?
   Daryl G. Smith

6. Student Goals for College and Courses: A Missing Link in Assessing and Improving Academic Achievement
   Joan S. Stark, Kathleen M. Shaw, and Malcolm A. Lowther

7. The Student as Commuter: Developing a Comprehensive Institutional Response
   Barbara Jacoby

8. Renewing Civic Capacity: Preparing College Students for Service and Citizenship
   Suzanne W. Morse

1988 ASHE-ERIC Higher Education Reports

1. The Invisible Tapestry: Culture in American Colleges and Universities
   George D. Kuh and Elizabeth J. Whitt

2. Critical Thinking: Theory, Research, Practice, and Possibilities
   Joanne Gainen Kurfiss

3. Developing Academic Programs: The Climate for Innovation
   Daniel T. Seymour

4. Peer Teaching: To Teach is To Learn Twice
   Neal A. Whitman

5. Higher Education and State Governments: Renewed Partnership, Cooperation, or Competition?
   Edward R. Hines

6. Entrepreneurship and Higher Education: Lessons for Colleges, Universities, and Industry
   James S. Fairweather

7. Planning for Microcomputers in Higher Education: Strategies for the Next Generation
   Reynolds Ferrante, John Hayman, Mary Susan Carlson, and Harry Phillips

8. The Challenge for Research in Higher Education: Harmonizing Excellence and Utility
   Alan W. Lindsay and Ruth T. Neumann

1987 ASHE-ERIC Higher Education Reports

1. Incentive Early Retirement Programs for Faculty: Innovative Responses to a Changing Environment
   Jay L. Chronister and Thomas R. Kepple, Jr.

2. Working Effectively with Trustees: Building Cooperative Campus Leadership
   Barbara E. Taylor

3. Formal Recognition of Employer-Sponsored Instruction: Conflict and Collegiality in Postsecondary Education
   Nancy S. Nash and Elizabeth M. Hawthorne

4. Learning Styles: Implications for Improving Educational Practices
   Charles S. Claxton and Patricia H. Murrell

5. Higher Education Leadership: Enhancing Skills through Professional Development Programs
   Sharon A. McDade

6. Higher Education and the Public Trust: Improving Stature in Colleges and Universities
   Richard L. Alfred and Julie Weissman

7. College Student Outcomes Assessment: A Talent Development Perspective
   Maryann Jacobi, Alexander Astin, and Frank Ayala, Jr.

8. Opportunity from Strength: Strategic Planning Clarified with Case Examples
   Robert G. Cope

1986 ASHE-ERIC Higher Education Reports

1. Post-tenure Faculty Evaluation: Threat or Opportunity?
   Christine M. Licata

2. Blue Ribbon Commissions and Higher Education: Changing Academe from the Outside
   Janet R. Johnson and Laurence R. Marcus

3. Responsive Professional Education: Balancing Outcomes and Opportunities
   Joan S. Stark, Malcolm A. Lowther, and Bonnie M.K. Hagerty

4. Increasing Students' Learning: A Faculty Guide to Reducing Stress among Students
   Neal A. Whitman, David C. Spendlove, and Claire H. Clark

5. Student Financial Aid and Women: Equity Dilemma?
   Mary Moran

6. The Master's Degree: Tradition, Diversity, Innovation
   Judith S. Glazer

7. The College, the Constitution, and the Consumer Student: Implications for Policy and Practice
   Robert M. Hendrickson and Annette Gibbs

8. Selecting College and University Personnel: The Quest and the Question
   Richard A. Kaplowitz

1985 ASHE-ERIC Higher Education Reports

1. Flexibility in Academic Staffing: Effective Policies and Practices
   Kenneth P. Mortimer, Marque Bagshaw, and Andrew T. Masland

2. Associations in Action: The Washington, D.C. Higher Education Community
   Harland G. Bloland

3. And on the Seventh Day: Faculty Consulting and Supplemental Income
   Carol M. Boyer and Darrell R. Lewis

4. Faculty Research Performance: Lessons from the Sciences and Social Sciences
   John W. Creswell

5. Academic Program Review: Institutional Approaches, Expectations, and Controversies
   Clifton F. Conrad and Richard F. Wilson

6. Students in Urban Settings: Achieving the Baccalaureate Degree
   Richard C. Richardson, Jr. and Louis W. Bender

7. Serving More Than Students: A Critical Need for College Student Personnel Services
   Peter H. Garland

8. Faculty Participation in Decision Making: Necessity or Luxury?
   Carol E. Floyd

1984 ASHE-ERIC Higher Education Reports

1. Adult Learning: State Policies and Institutional Practices
   K. Patricia Cross and Anne-Marie McCartan

2. Student Stress: Effects and Solutions
   Neal A. Whitman, David C. Spendlove, and Claire H. Clark

3. Part-time Faulty: Higher Education at a Crossroads
   Judith M. Gappa

4. Sex Discrimination Law in Higher Education: The Lessons of
   the Past Decade
   *J. Ralph Lindgren, Patti T. Ota, Perry A. Zirkel, and Nan Van
   Gieson*

5. Faculty Freedoms and Institutional Accountability: Interactions
   and Conflicts
   Steven G. Olswang and Barbara A. Lee

6. The High Technology Connection: Academic/Industrial Cooperation for Economic Growth
   Lynn G. Johnson

7. Employee Educational Programs: Implications for Industry and
   Higher Education
   Suzanne W. Morse

8. Academic Libraries: The Changing Knowledge Centers of Colleges and Universities
   Barbara B. Moran

9. Futures Research and the Strategic Planning Process: Implications for Higher Education
   James L. Morrison, William L. Renfro, and Wayne I. Boucher

10. Faculty Workload: Research, Theory, and Interpretation
    Harold E. Yuker

1983 ASHE-ERIC Higher Education Reports

1. The Path to Excellence: Quality Assurance in Higher Education
   Laurence R. Marcus, Anita O. Leone, and Edward D. Goldberg

2. Faculty Recruitment, Retention, and Fair Employment: Obligations and Opportunities
   John S. Waggaman

3. Meeting the Challenges: Developing Faculty Careers*
   Michael C.T. Brooks and Katherine L. German

4. Raising Academic Standards: A Guide to Learning Improvement
   Ruth Talbott Keimig

5. Serving Learners at a Distance: A Guide to Program Practices
   Charles E. Feasley

6. Competence, Admissions, and Articulation: Returning to the
   Basics in Higher Education
   Jean L. Preer

7. Public Service in Higher Education: Practices and Priorities
   Patricia H. Crosson

*Out-of-print. Available through EDRS. Call 1-800-227-ERIC.